KU-826-911

Contents

Introduction to Block 7

Prepared for the course team by Nicola J. Watson

You are now nearing the end of your work on the transition from Enlightenment to Romanticism. No account of the period would, however, be complete without a sense of how Europeans viewed non-Europeans. You have already had a taste of this in your study of Mungo Park's writings about Africa in Block 3, Units 12–13, and we shall extend that work in this, the last part of the course, which focuses on some of the ways in which Europeans of the period imagined the East – or, as they were more inclined to call it, 'the Orient'. In particular, we shall consider how fantasies of the East were integral to the construction of Romantic modes of being.

In Unit 31, Nicola Watson considers the building of the Royal Pavilion at Brighton, commissioned by the Prince of Wales in 1787 and completed in 1823, analysing it as a Romantic fantasy of the East in the service of the prince's desire to display his own subjectivity and dramatize a certain type of monarchical power. In Unit 32, Linda Walsh turns to examine the career and work of the French painter Ferdinand-Victor-Eugène Delacroix (1798–1863), considering his engagement with the Oriental and the exotic as a subject and an aesthetic that would allow for technical and intellectual innovation. The discussion in that unit largely revolves around Delacroix's important and controversial canvas, *The Death of Sardanapalus* (1827–8). The accompanying video extends this discussion to two more of Delacroix's paintings, both entitled *Women of Algiers* (1834 and 1849). Both units thus deal with highly innovatory works of art, relating that innovation to the Romantic temper and in particular to its 'take' on the East. The block as a whole contrasts an art practised under a royal connoisseur's patronage in England with an art practised under the very different conditions obtaining in restoration France. Both forms turn out to be bound up as much with contemporary politics at home as with fantasies of abroad. The two case studies also chronicle the uncertain and uneven ways in which the classical and neoclassical metamorphosed into the Romantic, the pressures that forced and enabled that aesthetic transition, and the ways in which contemporaries, including Delacroix, had mixed feelings about their own modernity.

Our aims in Block 7 are:

1   to examine two innovatory works of art in detail – the Royal Pavilion at Brighton and *The Death of Sardanapalus*;

2   to locate these works within their intellectual, political and aesthetic contexts;

3   in particular, to relate these works to notions of the 'Romantic' in the period;

4   to explain and explore more generally the aesthetic opportunities
     which the Romantic found in ideas about 'the Orient' that were
     common in the period.

For Enlightenment and Romantic culture alike, the East was curiously
unbound by geographical or even political realities. In defiance of
geography, the 'Oriental' might be taken to mean the far reaches of
eastern Europe, the Middle East and/or parts of Africa, India or China.
The availability of the East as an aesthetic or imaginative territory was
certainly mapped by political realities and trade routes. For instance,
Brighton Pavilion's 'East' is noticeably Chinese and Indian, reflecting
Britain's longstanding trading interests in China and India throughout the
eighteenth century, while Delacroix's paintings demonstrate a strong bias
towards the Middle East and North Africa, reflecting Napoleon's
campaigns in Egypt and ongoing French interests in the area. Yet, for the
Romantics, the East remained remarkably unspecific, and Delacroix and
the Prince of Wales shared a surprisingly similar sense of the Orient.

Enlightenment culture had long had a strong interest in the East. Political
satires often used the conceit of letters from Persians, 'Hindoos' or the
Chinese to point up the follies and failings of their own societies, as in
Montesquieu's *Persian Letters* (1721) or Oliver Goldsmith's *The Citizen of
the World* (1762). Travel writers wrote proto-anthropological accounts of
eastern societies as part of the encyclopaedic thirst for knowledge and
classification, but also as part of a general analysis of the superiority of
an enlightened civilization. Painters and decorative artists imported
motifs from the East to enliven and enrich the interiors they designed for
the wealthy. But, sometime around the late 1780s, a change made itself
felt, for which little satisfactory explanation has so far been provided.

The eighteenth century had always identified an element of fantasy
(often sexual fantasy) within the idea of the East. For instance,
entrepreneurs and decorators had provided examples of that tasteful
fantasy as a backdrop for assignations in outdoor pleasure-grounds such
as Vauxhall in London, while the notion occasionally provided the
background for erotic fiction, as in Diderot's *Indiscreet Jewels* (1748). It
was also commonplace to dress for the louche delights of the
masquerade in the guise of an eastern sultan or harem beauty. But at the
end of the 1700s this element of fantasy assumed much greater
prominence in the notion of 'the East'. If early Enlightenment culture had
looked to the foreign and divided it into the 'civilized' (China) and the
'barbarian' (most of Africa, Hindu India and sometimes, but not always,
Islam), the newborn Romantic eye saw in it a difference and a mystery
that licensed otherwise forbidden fantasy, illicit desire and extreme
experimentation. While the Enlightenment saw the Orient as a place that
could be known through travel and scientific observation, the Romantics
delighted in its unknowability – which gave scope for self-exploration
and self-expression outside the confines of the acceptable. Ultimately
inscrutable, only partially apprehensible through a barrier of unfamiliar

dress, language, religion and social expectations, the East was hospitable to the Romantic hunger for the sublime. Dressed up in a turban or dressed down in a sari, it was possible to explore transgressive types of sexual desire, violence and self-aggrandizement, possible to live more intensely, enfolded in the grotesque and the bizarre, the esoteric and the highly coloured. Above all, it was possible to escape present-day wartime and post-war reality. To this desire we can in part attribute the best-sellerdom of Byron's poetic 'Oriental tales', especially *The Giaour* (1813) – so successful in surrounding the poet with an aura of sexy celebrity that he cashed in on it with one of the most famous portraits of him, depicting him in Oriental fancy dress (see Plate 29.7 in the Illustrations Book). This is not to say that this impulse wasn't on occasion criticized and mocked – far from it. Maria Edgeworth efficiently satirized this yen in her novel *The Absentee* (1812), which portrays a party held by a social climber, complete with furniture and decor borrowed from the Orient. The immediate petty social concerns of the women in the book, evidenced by their malice and their efforts at one-upmanship, puncture the imaginative glamour and social fluidity aspired to by the eastern decor. Although the Prince Regent never travelled to the East except in his imagination, Delacroix did make a trip to Morocco which enabled him to compare European ideas of the East with the reality. The video that accompanies the unit on Delacroix explores how far his travels modified his vision of eastern decadence expressed in *The Death of Sardanapalus* by looking at his later *Women of Algiers* paintings.

As well as examining how the Prince of Wales and Delacroix responded to the imaginative pull of the East, we have tried here to provide a detailed context for each subject, setting out some biographical details within a sense of the contemporary intellectual, political and economic environments. In the case of the Pavilion, this involves a consideration of the personality of the Prince of Wales, his political relation to the establishment, his investment in the idea of the 'man of taste', the ways in which it was possible to fund the Pavilion, and contemporary reactions to the building. In the case of Delacroix, this mandates a consideration of his career as a whole, the ways in which he endeavoured to position himself in relation to the art establishment, a consideration of his innovations and theoretical writings, and an analysis of contemporary responses to his work.

Unit 31
The Royal Pavilion at Brighton

Prepared for the course team by Nicola J. Watson

Contents

Study components

Weeks of study	Supplementary material	Audio-visual	Anthologies and set books
1½	AV Notes Illustrations Book	Video 4	Anthology II

Objectives

By the end of this unit, you should have:

- acquired a critical vocabulary suitable to the analysis of Regency architecture, interior decor and garden design;
- further developed your sense of the continuities and differences between neoclassical Enlightenment architecture and Romantic architecture;
- developed a sense of the history of fantastic architecture and garden architecture in the late eighteenth and early nineteenth centuries;
- come to an understanding of the varied social and political meanings of such architecture;
- developed a sense of what constitutes the 'Romantic' in both architecture and literature, and come to a further refinement of your ideas about Romanticism.

1 Introduction

In this unit we shall be studying a quintessentially Romantic piece of architecture, the Royal Pavilion at Brighton, designed and redesigned over the course of some 30 years to the specifications of the Prince of Wales, afterwards Prince Regent and eventually King George IV (1762–1830; reigned 1820–30). The Pavilion as we now know it in its final state was the result of a collaboration between the architect Sir John Nash (1752–1835), the firm of Crace (specialists in interior decoration) and their patron the Prince Regent. It makes a suggestive companion piece to the house of Sir John Soane that you have already studied in Block 5, Units 22–23. Although both buildings are markedly personal in cast, Soane's house can be regarded as a Romantic 'take' on Enlightenment classicism, while the Pavilion could be called a Regency 'take' on the Romantic (what I mean by this distinction will become clearer as we progress). Whereas Soane's house celebrates the architect as sole creator, the Pavilion is much more typically the product of a collaboration between architect and client. While Soane was and is the architect's architect, an intellectual and an academic, distinguished, original and serious, Nash was the darling of fashionable aristocratic society, careless, humorous and audacious in style, and was and is identified with the commercial and the opportunistic. Where Soane is essentially a purist, refining and romanticizing Neoclassicism, Nash is associated with eclecticism, which by contrast privileges asymmetry and recklessly mixes forms, motifs and details from different historical periods and styles.

The Pavilion itself has been called silly, charming, witty, light-hearted, extravagant, gloriously eccentric, decadent, childish, painfully vulgar, socially irresponsible, a piece of outrageous folly and a stylistic phantasmagoria. Whatever you decide about it, it has always been, beyond all dispute, an astonishing flight of the Romantic fancy, comparable in its impulse to Samuel Taylor Coleridge's famous poem 'Kubla Khan' (drafted 1798, published 1816, available to read in its entirety in Anthology II, pp.359–60). The poem begins:

> In Xanadu did KUBLA KHAN
> A stately pleasure-dome decree:
> Where ALPH, the sacred river, ran
> Through caverns measureless to man
> Down to a sunless sea.

Coleridge's poem did not in itself influence the building of the Pavilion, but both 'Kubla Khan' and the Pavilion do recognizably grow out of a common stock of Romantic ideas and feelings about the Orient. Here we shall be trying to come to some understanding of how, why and to what effect the prince's 'pleasure-dome' translated some of the modes and ideas of Romanticism into the language of architecture. As we do so, we'll be thinking about the Pavilion as what we might call a 'cultural formation'. By this I mean that considering the apparent eccentricity of this building can give us an insight into many aspects of Regency culture, and, conversely, that an enhanced knowledge of Regency culture can help us to decode the meanings of the building for its own time. The Pavilion can be seen as the physical realization of the coming together of many aspects of Regency society: systems of patronage of the arts; ideas of health, leisure and pleasure; notions of technological progress, which drove the Industrial Revolution and were in turn reinforced by it; concepts of public and private and the proper relations between them; ideas of royal authority in the post-Napoleonic era of restoration of hereditary monarchies across Europe; the fashion for Oriental scholarship and the 'Oriental tale'; and powerfully interconnected ideas of trade, empire and the East. By the end of the unit, therefore, you will, I hope, have developed a sense of some of the (sometimes contradictory) values dramatized by Romantic exoticism.

Before we can talk about the meanings of the Pavilion in its own time, however, you will need to familiarize yourself with the building. On Video 4, band 2, *The Royal Pavilion, Brighton*, you will find a virtual tour of the Pavilion, inside and out. The video is structured as though you were a visitor to the Pavilion in the early 1820s. You will trace the route through the rooms that you would have followed if you were arriving as a guest at one of the prince's famous evening receptions, consisting of dinner followed by music. You will hear on the sound-track the music that the prince loved, together with some of the comments of his guests, and extracts from contemporary descriptions of the Pavilion's interior from a newspaper and a guidebook.

EXERCISE   Read the accompanying AV Notes and then watch the video carefully once through. Concentrate principally on the look of the exterior and of the interiors. Then I suggest you watch the video again, following your route on the modern ground-floor plan provided here (Figure 31.1), and looking carefully at the contemporary watercolours of exteriors and interiors provided in the Illustrations Book (Plates 31.1–31.11).

Once you have done this, compile a list of adjectives that occur to you to describe your experience of the building, both exterior and interior. Bearing in mind your earlier work on Sir John Soane's house, you might also like to add to your list some phrases describing those effects in which this building is conspicuously *not* interested.

DISCUSSION   I don't expect that our lists will match exactly – but we might agree roughly on some of the effects that the building produces on us. What I've noted down is that the exterior strikes me as definitely 'Indian' – in fact, vaguely reminiscent of the Taj Mahal. The Entrance Hall, the Long Gallery and the Saloon are clearly 'Chinese', and so are the Banqueting

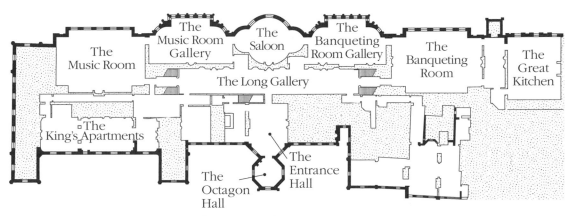

Figure 31.1   Modern ground-floor plan of the Royal Pavilion, Brighton. Adapted from Jessica M.F. Rutherford, The Royal Pavilion, *1995, courtesy of the Royal Pavilion, Libraries and Museums, Brighton and Hove.*

Room and Music Room, although they are Chinese (with a dash of 'Indian'?) in a rather different and much more grandiose mode. (Don't worry if you found it hard to put your finger on the exact difference in style; we'll be unpicking these Indian and Chinese effects in more detail a little later.)

After that, I have a list of descriptive terms that runs something like this: conspicuously expensive; sumptuously detailed to the suffocating edge of over-kill; self-advertising; highly personal, fantastic and esoterically refined; spectacular, theatrical and faintly reminiscent of some of the pleasures of Disneyland's evocations of foreign parts; sensual to the point of overwhelming the senses; and, related to this, disorientating (all those mirrors and all that **trompe l'oeil**); an escapist pocket palace.

As for what this building is *not* trying to do or be – it is spectacularly not invested in neoclassical politeness, nor in antiquities or other sorts of collectables. (To test this assertion for yourself, compare the effects that Soane's house tries to achieve.) The Pavilion is profoundly uninterested in the past, the nation or conventional domesticity, in respectability, or in social responsibility, or in work of any sort. Related to this last point, it is conspicuously not the centrepiece of landed wealth – it is not standing in a place of eminence, embedded within its own estate and associated farms which would be visibly providing the income for the upkeep of the house (you might think back here to Video 3, band 1 about the politics of gardens that you saw in conjunction with your study of the Lake District in Block 4, Units 16 and 17). Carrying this thought a little further suggests forcibly that the wealth this palace is designed to display is a wealth of **taste** and *imagination*. Above all, this building is *surprising*.

Actually, I'd go further than this – I think this building is astonishing, and its sheer improbability generates in me a curiosity about the circumstances that could conceivably have made it possible.

EXERCISE   Now I want you to try to formulate a set of questions that the Pavilion might prompt about the culture that produced it. To this set of questions, I should like you to add a list of the sorts of information you would need to collect about that culture so as to be able to answer them. (If you are feeling especially imaginative and adventurous, you might like to write yet another list of suggestions as to where you might start looking for this sort of information.)

DISCUSSION   My list of initial questions looks like this (again, it won't match yours exactly or perhaps even at all, and you shouldn't worry about that):

1   Why was the Prince of Wales building a palace in Brighton at all?

2   For what was the Pavilion intended and used, and for how long?

3   When and why did he choose this style of exotic architecture and interior decor?

4   Why is the Pavilion 'Chinese' on the inside but 'Indian' on the outside?

5   What did everyone think about it at the time?

My second list, of information I would need to collect so as to begin to answer these questions, runs as follows:

1   Find out about the Prince of Wales – e.g. his other residences, his relations with his father's court in London, where his money was coming from, and where he got the idea for the Pavilion (try biographies, books on court history).

2   Find out about Brighton and why it had become fashionable at this juncture – at a guess, it must have been fashionable for the prince to have ended up there (start with histories of Brighton, and eighteenth-century, early nineteenth-century and modern guidebooks to the city).

3   Find out something about the history of the building of the Pavilion (again, try guidebooks old and new and see what leads come up; also see whether rival architects published sketches and ground-plans to support their bids for the work).

4   Find out whether there were any earlier or other contemporary buildings that were 'exotic' in this style. Perhaps there were architects/interior designers who specialized in this sort of work? Possibly as part of a long tradition in such designs? Or was this style a fashion that was echoed across the period in, say, literature and

painting? (Try books about architecture, or studies of the Romantic exotic more generally.)

5   Find out who were the prince's visitors to the Pavilion, and see if they wrote letters or diaries describing their visits. The same might apply for prominent writers who were visitors to Brighton. Check, too, for political caricatures of the prince that might comment on his building of the Pavilion.

What I've just done, as you can see, is to write out a rough programme for research. In fact I followed this programme in order to write what follows, and I hope you will enjoy following me step by step through what I discovered – and deciding whether you agree with my judgements.

2   A prince at the seaside

The Prince of Wales (see Figure 31.2), known familiarly to his friends as 'Prinny', was born in 1762 and destined to become Prince Regent in 1811 following the onset of the madness of his father, George III. He finally became George IV in 1820, but reigned as such for only a decade, dying in 1830 at the age of 68. He is remembered as a great connoisseur and collector of art (setting a precedent for subsequent Princes of Wales to take an interest in architecture), most especially through his patronage of John Nash, who at his behest redesigned Buckingham Palace and created the elegant London developments still known as Regent Street and Regent's Park. Handsome, intelligent and accomplished, the prince was also highly emotional, duplicitous, painfully susceptible to flattery, wildly extravagant, greedy for excitement and personally theatrical. The Princess Lieven, wife of Tsar Alexander I's ambassador and a notable judge of character, described him as he was in the 1820s, as having 'some wit, and great penetration':

> he quickly summed up persons and things; he was educated and had much tact, easy, animated and varied conversation, not at all pedantic. He adorned the subjects he touched, he knew how to listen, he was very polished ... also affectionate, sympathetic, and galant. But he was full of vanity, and could be flattered at will. Weary of all the joys of life, having only taste, not one true sentiment, he was hardly susceptible to attachment, and never I believe sincerely inspired anybody with it.
>
> (Temperley, 1930, p.119)

In early life the prince was also breathtakingly indiscreet, both in his youthful politics (he was a hard-core oppositional Whig rather than

Figure 31.2   Sir Thomas Lawrence, George IV as Prince Regent, *c.1814, oil on canvas, 91.4 x 71.1 cm, National Portrait Gallery, London. Photo: courtesy of the National Portrait Gallery, London.*

favouring the establishment party, the Tories, supported by his father) and in his youthful love affairs (which were many and various, culminating in the scandal of his private, unacknowledged, unconstitutional and therefore unlawful marriage to the Roman Catholic widow, Mrs Fitzherbert). As a result, and as so many heirs to the throne have done, during his twenties and thirties the prince enjoyed a strained relation with his father's court, which he found staid and stifling. His form of rebellion was to combine spendthrift dissoluteness (hence the anonymous print of 1787 depicting the prince as the Prodigal Son; see Figure 31.3) with the life of an aesthete, which found expression in the court he held at Carlton House. His set of associates included dandies such as Beau Brummell (who affected beautiful, consciously urban clothes and a pose of bored languor as he strolled up and down the Mall), sporting rakes like the Duke of Queensberry, and high-class courtesans such as Harriette Wilson. These were blended with society literati such as the playwright Richard Brinsley Sheridan, the millionaire connoisseur William Beckford (author of the torrid Oriental fiction *Vathek: An Arabian Tale* (1786), who purchased the famous statue of Napoleon pulled down – as you will remember from Stendhal's account in Block 2, Units 7–8 – from the Vendôme Column), and the best-selling poet Thomas Moore, shot to fame by the success of his long Oriental romance poem *Lalla Rookh* (1817).

Carlton House, sumptuously decorated in the height of fashionable Francophile taste in line with the prince's Whig sympathies by the important architect Henry Holland (1745–1806), was the setting for a

Figure 31.3   Anonymous (probably Henry Kingsbury), The Prodigal Son*, 1787, drawing. Photo: courtesy of the Royal Pavilion, Libraries and Museums, Brighton and Hove.*

The Prodigal Son features in a parable related in the Bible as a delinquent son welcomed back by his father when he repents of his ways.

series of the extravagant parties which the prince so loved to give, culminating in the famous Carlton House fête in 1811 on his appointment as Regent. The dazzled Thomas Moore wrote to his mother about this fête, detailing the delights of the indoor fountain and the artificial brook that ran down the centre of the table, and concluding, 'Nothing was ever half so magnificent. It was in *reality* all that they try to imitate in the gorgeous scenery of the theatre' (quoted in Hibbert, 1973, p.371). Byron's friend and fellow radical poet Percy Bysshe Shelley, by contrast, was predictably outraged by the cost (see Hibbert, 1973, p.374). In the event Carlton House, with its rival court, did not prove far enough removed from his father to suit the young heir. Instead he would lure his raffish and brilliant society, with its love of extravagance and theatricality, out of the capital and down to the margins of the nation, to a place then called Brighthelmstone, some eight hours away by stage-coach (although in 1784 the prince achieved the journey in four and a half hours for a bet).

The Prince of Wales first visited Brighton (short for Brighthelmstone) in 1783, aged 21, staying with his uncle at Grove House on the Steine (or Steyne), a broad street that led from the seafront into the heart of town (see Figure 31.4). He was prompted partly by his ever-lively desire to escape the disapproving eyes of his father's court, and partly by the recommendation of his physicians, who suggested that sea water might ease the glandular swellings in his neck. This sea-water cure had been the original cause of the rise in the popularity of Brighton as a watering place, which had started around 1765, courtesy of a Dr Richard Russell of Lewes who had publicized the health-giving properties of bathing in, and drinking, sea water in his *A Dissertation: Concerning the Use of Sea Water in Diseases of the Glands, etc.* (1752). Sea water taken one way or another, according to Russell, would cure almost any disease, including 'fluxions of redundant humours', rheumatism, madness, consumption, impotence, rabies and childish ailments. Among the early visitors was Dr Johnson, but it was soon to become a resort for the fashionable as well. As one wag was to put it, high society 'Rush'd coastward to be cur'd like tongues/By dipping into brine' (unattributed, quoted in Roberts, 1939, p.3), or turned out to spy through telescopes on 'mad Naiads in flannel smocks' as they emerged briefly from their bathing machines (Pasquin, 1796, p.5).

These health treatments, generally undertaken after the rigours of the London season which ran from March until June, were much sweetened by the other pleasures that Brighton had on offer besides the beauties of nature. They included a racecourse, hunting, circulating libraries, promenading and ogling along the Parade, donkey-rides on the beach, balls and assemblies at the Old Ship and the Castle Inn, and the theatre, where you might have seen the celebrated actresses Mrs Siddons and Mrs Jordan. (The new Theatre Royal at Brighton was soon able to attract such London celebrity performers not just during the summer, when the London theatres were closed, but over the Christmas season too.) This

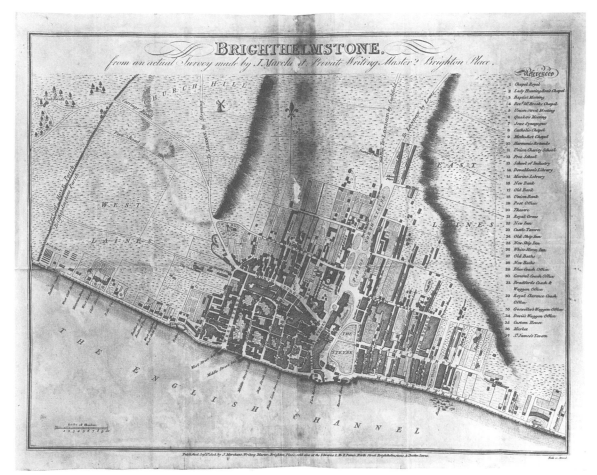

Figure 31.4   Map of Brighthelmstone, frontispiece from H.R. Attree, Topography of Brighton: and, Picture of the Roads, from Thence to the Metropolis, *London, 1809. Photo: Bodleian Library, University of Oxford (G.A. Sussex 8° 22).*

landscape came complete with figures – rakes, parvenus, the frail lovelies of the so-called 'Cyprian corps' (a Regency euphemism for prostitutes, derived ultimately from the classical myth that Venus was born naked from the waves at Cyprus) and officers from the nearby military camp. The army came under the prince's personal command in his capacity as commander-in-chief, and many officers were his intimates; the arrival of the military therefore sealed the glamorous image of the resort. As Jane Austen was to write in *Pride and Prejudice* (1813):

> In Lydia's imagination a visit to Brighton comprized every possibility of earthly happiness. She saw with the creative eye of fancy, the streets of that gay bathing-place covered with officers. She saw herself the object of attention to tens and scores of them at present unknown ... she saw herself seated beneath a tent, tenderly flirting with at least six officers at once.

(Austen, 1967, p.232)

This invasion of London raffishness prompted the occasional fierce satire. Anthony Pasquin's poetic *The New Brighton Guide* (1796) describes Brighton in a note as

> one of those numerous watering-places which beskirt this polluted island, and operate as apologies for idleness, sensuality, and nearly all the ramifications of social imposture ... where the voluptuary [secks] to wash the cobwebs from the interstices of his flaccid anatomy.
>
> (Pasquin, 1796, p.5)

The painter Constable sourly described Brighton as 'Piccadilly or worse by the sea' and 'the receptacle of the fashion and off-scouring of London' (quoted in Leslie, 1951, p.123). But the prevailing view of Brighton was that, unlike more established resorts, it offered a picturesque, even a virtuously Rousseauesque, rustic informality, allowing visitors to escape the constrictions and excesses of life in town to partake of 'pure air, rational amusement, and sea-bathing' (Fisher, 1800, p.viii). As Mary Lloyd put it in her *Brighton: A Poem*, it was

> a pleasing gay Retreat,
> Beauty, and fashion's ever favourite seat:
> Where splendour lays its cumbrous pomps aside,
> Content in softer, simpler paths to glide.
>
> (Lloyd, 1809, p.4)

This agreeable vision owed a good deal to the Prince of Wales himself, who both set the seal of fashionability upon Brighton (relegating its rivals, Bath and Tunbridge Wells, to middle-class dowdiness) and did much to exploit and reinforce this cult of Romantic love-in-a-cottage – to begin with, at least. Having rented a picturesque farmhouse on the Steine in 1784 for a couple of years, he determined in 1786 to reform, retrench and retire to Brighton, installing his new wife Mrs Fitzherbert just around the corner, there to live a life of simple, if self-dramatizing, poverty (see Figure 31.5). Strict economy notwithstanding, he commissioned his then favourite architect Henry Holland to convert the farmhouse into a gentleman's residence with good views of the sea and the Steine. Rebuilt in the early summer of 1787, it would come to be called the Marine Pavilion.

EXERCISE   Look carefully at the two prints which show the Marine Pavilion in 1787 and 1796 (Figure 31.6 here, p.22, and Plate 31.12 in the Illustrations Book), at the ground-floor plan of Holland's Marine Pavilion (Figure 31.7, p.22), and at the watercolour which shows the interior decorative scheme of the Saloon *c*.1789 (Plate 31.13). I should like you to make some notes along the following lines:

Figure 31.5   Anonymous, Love's Last Shift, *published 1787 by S.W. Fores, London. Photo: courtesy of the Royal Pavilion, Libraries and Museums, Brighton and Hove.*

1   Describe some of the architectural features (both exterior and interior) that strike you.

2   Remembering your work on Sir John Soane's house (see Block 5, Units 22–23), make a stab at identifying the architectural styles that this building evokes.

3   Consider the house's relation to its setting.

4   Consider what your observations might tell you about the young prince's vision of his life in Brighton.

5   Speculate on what the prince may have been intending to suggest by calling his newly modelled house a 'pavilion'. (Here you might find it illuminating to consult the *Oxford English Dictionary*.)[1]

DISCUSSION   1   Holland's Marine Pavilion is notably *symmetrical* in conception. The original farmhouse has vanished into the left-hand wing of the new structure, which is now mirrored by an identical right-hand wing with matching bays. The composition is centred on a domed **rotunda** fronted by slender Ionic columns. The building is whitish, unlike the surrounding brick buildings. The same symmetry is visible in Thomas Rowlandson's depiction of the interior of the Pavilion

[1] This is available online through your eDesktop.

Figure 31.6   Samuel H. Grimm, The Prince of Wales' Pavilion at Brighthelmstone, from the Steyne, *1787, British Library, London. Photo: by permission of the British Library, London.*

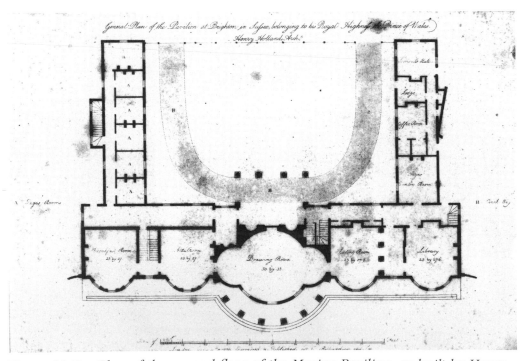

Figure 31.7   Plan of the ground floor of the Marine Pavilion, as built by Henry Holland, 1796, engraved and published by G. Richardson and Son. Photo: courtesy of the Royal Pavilion, Libraries and Museums, Brighton and Hove.

(Plate 31.13). Mirror is balanced by mirror, seat by seat and fireplace by console. The plasterwork is uniform, and repeated in panel after panel and in the **coffering** of the ceiling.

2   The rotunda (and its columns) make clear reference to classical civilization. It is Roman in its evocation of the Pantheon (a building you have already studied in your work on Soane) and Greek in its Ionic columns. This Neoclassicism is further underlined by Holland's decision to clad the whole building in cream-glazed Hampshire tiles, mimicking the paleness of marble. The symmetry visible in the interior of the rotunda is similarly neoclassical. This scheme is also derived – via the interior designer Robert Adam (1728–92) – from the coffered interior of the Pantheon.

3   The Pavilion is orientated very strongly towards the main street on which it is located (the Steine) and therefore to taking part in the social display that was such a feature of this area. The house combines both modesty and grandeur: it is almost aggressively modest in height in relation to the other buildings around it, but at the same time it makes no effort to blend in with them.

4   The building suggests that the prince saw himself while sojourning in Brighton as passing incognito, disguised as a commoner. But at the same time it also suggests that the prince's disguise was meant to be penetrated; he might have been living in virtuous poverty, but this was poverty in the most sophisticated taste, poverty as fashion statement, poverty as a holiday from inborn and inalienable royal importance.

5   There is much to be deduced from a name. By calling his house a 'pavilion' – a term, according to the *Oxford English Dictionary*, which at this period (the 1780s) meant exclusively an Oriental tent, a temporary and moveable outdoor dwelling – the prince was invoking a striking series of connotations: of temporariness, of holiday and of fantasy escape. (In fact, the rotunda does have something of the appearance of a tent-like structure, and the architect Humphrey Repton (1752–1810) compared the interior effect to that of a marquee (see Dinkel, 1983, p.20).)

On the one hand, then, this building is thoroughly conventional. This sort of neoclassical architecture was an eighteenth-century Enlightenment shorthand for belonging to a well-heeled, cosmopolitan Whig landowner. The whole – dignified, sumptuous, but quite subdued in effect – is depicted by Thomas Rowlandson as populated with figures engaged in the polite and formalized conversation of good society (see Plate 31.13). On the other hand, the prince's retreat was founded in a fantasy of 'dropping out'. The restless owner would not long remain content with this version of his Pavilion; but at its core through all its transformations

lay a notion of self-dramatizing metamorphosis and of temporary,
alternative and essentially irresponsible experience undertaken incognito.
(An incident from the prince's early life is particularly telling here; in his
twenties he fell for the beautiful actress Mary Robinson in the role of
Perdita in Shakespeare's late romance *The Winter's Tale*. Perdita is
apparently a shepherdess but is actually a lost princess; she meets and
falls in love with Florizel, seemingly a shepherd but in fact a prince in
disguise. Not for nothing were the couple promptly dubbed by London
society and by the caricaturists 'Florizel and Perdita' – the prince clearly
loved romantic slumming from very early on.)

3   From Enlightenment to Romantic?

In 1800, having divorced Mrs Fitzherbert and contracted a disastrous
marriage with Princess Caroline of Brunswick, forced on him by the
necessity of persuading the king to clear his vast debts, the Prince of
Wales fled back to Brighton with his court. In 1801 he whiled away his
time (and squandered Caroline's dowry) dreaming up extensions and
changes to the interior decor of the Pavilion.

Of these, certainly the most interesting and prophetic was his
development of the interior into a Chinese fantasy between 1802 and
1804, a development perhaps suggested by his fantasy of a 'pavilion' – a
term that by now was being applied to small garden buildings of a
Chinese style. He hung his newly decorated rooms with genuine Chinese
wallpaper sent from that country's imperial court and crammed them
with a collection of imported items supplied by the firm of Frederick
Crace & Sons. These ranged in promiscuous profusion from model
pagodas and carved ivory junks to birds' nests, Chinese razors, silks and
pieces of fine porcelain. Like Soane, he seems to have been taken with
the idea of displaying a collection of curiosities, mounting the rare and
the bizarre in witty and deliberately heterogeneous juxtaposition. Lady
Bessborough wrote of the effect in 1805: 'I did not think the strange
Chinese shapes and columns could have looked so well. It is like
Concetti[2] in Poetry, in outré and false taste, but for the kind of thing as
perfect as it can be' (see Anthology II, p.364).

It is important to understand, however, that the prince's liking for things
Chinese was not especially innovative. The rage for Chinese imports had
gone in and out of fashion throughout the late seventeenth and
eighteenth centuries as French and British traders had penetrated the
huge Chinese empire. The rich and aristocratic, leaders of fashion, had
typically amassed rare and beautiful objects from the Chinese export

---

[2] By 'Concetti' Lady Bessborough meant the elaborate 'conceits' (strained and
conspicuously witty metaphors that yoke unlikely things together) of the sort
characteristic of the lyrics of the seventeenth-century English poet John Donne.

market, most especially porcelain and silks, which embodied superior technological skills that to date had baffled the West. So important did Europe become as a market for these wares that the Chinese invented a special export market, designing on vases and bowls painted scenes purportedly of European life but in a distinctively Chinese style. This English liking for Chinese products spilled over into a variant of Rococo style around the 1740s. Known as **chinoiserie**, this influenced the design of textiles, furniture and gardens in courts and great houses across Europe, including one belonging to the Russian empress, Catherine the Great (1729–96). The 1780s and 1790s saw in particular a fad for Chinese gardening in a '**grotesque**' style. This resulted in the famous pagoda designed by Sir William Chambers (1726–92) for London's Kew Gardens, in Frederick the Great's Chinese-style tea-house at Sans-Souci in Germany (which features briefly in Video 1, band 1), and in the similar Chinese tea house in the grounds at Stowe in Buckinghamshire, all of which can still be seen if you care to visit them. Like the pleasures of the **Gothick** folly (exemplified in the building of Fonthill Abbey in Wiltshire by the prince's vastly rich friend, William Beckford), this sort of 'Chineseness' bore witness to a rebellious undercurrent that ran counter to, and in parallel with, established Neoclassicism, although for the most part safely located outside the house in the grounds. As John Dinkel puts it:

> Those essentially ornamental eye-stoppers, the innumerable sham Gothic ruins, pyramids, Turkish tents, pagodas, and Chinese tea-houses that sprinkled gentlemen's estates, were all fashionable expressions of the impulse to break the established rules of classical taste.
>
> (Dinkel, 1983, p.7)

Yet escaping into Chinese fantasy was, to the eighteenth-century mind, not an escape into the barbaric. The Chinese appeared to an Enlightenment eye to offer an alluring model of imperial stability, of gracious ritual and strict hierarchy, of wit, charming illusion, and the pleasures of narratives in miniature. The Chinese were supposed to be eminently *civilized*. This was one reason why Oliver Goldsmith's novel satirizing the follies of British society, *The Citizen of the World* (1762), took as its central figure a Chinese philosophic gentleman residing in London writing home in some bewilderment at the habits of the natives, and why Voltaire took the view that China was a sophisticated land of admirable stability peopled by *philosophes*. The connotations of China in the prince's day were, in short, those of luxury, gaiety and the trappings of rank (Dinkel, 1983, p.33), although increasingly towards the end of the eighteenth century this view was tempered by a sense that Chinese civilization was stagnant by comparison with the vigour of Enlightenment Europe.

The prince himself was not new to the pleasures of connoisseurship in this area; by 1790 Carlton House already boasted the famous Yellow

A VIEW OF THE PRINCE OF WALES'S CHINESE DRAWING ROOM.   Pl.32.

Figure 31.8   J. Barlow, after Thomas Sheraton, A View of the Prince of Wales's Chinese Drawing Room, *1792, engraving, from Thomas Sheraton,* Cabinet Maker & Upholsterer's Drawing Book, *British Library, London. Photo: by permission of the British Library, London (shelfmark 61.e.22).*

Drawing Room in the Chinese style (see Figure 31.8). At this time, Chinese taste was all the rage in 'advanced' circles. None the less, it was one thing to collect the occasional piece of beautiful china and the odd strip of hand-painted wallpaper, setting them in 'exotic' colour schemes, and quite another to collect pagodas, birds' nests, razors and vast amounts of china. The one was an exercise in graceful allusion, the other a demonstration of a witty taste for the grotesque and the bizarre, increasingly characteristic of turn-of-the-century Romantic taste.

EXERCISE   I'd like you to look carefully at Figure 31.8 and compare it with:

- Rowlandson's sketch of the original interior of the Saloon in the Marine Pavilion (Plate 31.13 in the Illustrations Book);

- the illustration of the Long Gallery, which shows a rather later decorating scheme designed by Frederick Crace around 1815 (Plate 31.5).

What, if anything, does the Yellow Drawing Room have in common with each of these schemes?

DISCUSSION   Clearly, all three designs do have in common an underlying concern with symmetry and balance, a thoroughly neoclassical and Enlightenment trait. But my own sense is that the Chineseness of the Yellow Drawing Room is more akin to the spirit of the sketch of the Saloon. It speaks of a cultivated taste, backed by plenty of money and leisure; it is decorative and witty, polite and, most important, formal, as befits a royal London residence. (The Saloon seems a little less formal in Rowlandson's conception – but then, it is part of a holiday house in a seaside resort.) By contrast, Crace's designs for the Long Gallery seem much more invested in alternative, exotic experience, perhaps straying outside the strictly polite. You may have noticed how the underlying neoclassical symmetries of the Long Gallery are broken, distorted and unsettled by the quite violent diagonals of the bamboo on the wallpaper, by the tiles that line the **coving**, mimicking a Chinese roof, and especially by the consciously 'foreign' lines of the cast-iron dragon columns that stand at each side of the passage. The colours are brilliant, and flamboyantly and unconventionally combined. The effect is akin to the idea of the picturesque that you studied in Block 4, Units 16 and 17: it privileges a roughness, a serpentine line, 'variety' and the power of a framed perspective. It is a theatrical experience – which perhaps is not so very surprising given that the Long Gallery (unlike the Saloon) was for looking down and walking through rather than sitting in.

What the differences between these interior schemes suggest to me is that by 1815 the prince's earlier 'Enlightenment' taste for chinoiserie had metamorphosed into something more 'Romantic', something less congruent with neoclassical order, balance and symmetry. That slight but definite tinge of the bizarre suggested by the collection of birds' nests in 1802 would be much elaborated by the prince and his designers over the first two decades of the nineteenth century.

At the turn of the century, the governing idea of a 'man of taste' was changing. Whereas, as we noted in Units 16 and 17, during the eighteenth century such a man would have been concerned to display his genealogy, his wealth and his classical education topped off with Grand Tour souvenirs in his house, he now invented himself by creating something strange and personal; hence the fantasy-world interiors of Beckford and Soane, 'hungry for thrilling sensations evoked by ancient and Eastern artefacts' (Dinkel, 1983, p.8). This intensely personal and sensational fantasy would become a hallmark of Regency, and Romantic, style. Dandyism in taste, and the ascendancy of the most famous dandy of them all, Beau Brummell, for several years the prince's boon-companion, was only just around the corner. The Pavilion's Chinese interiors, therefore, were to the prince an expression of Romantic subjectivity, a crystallization of his sense, shared by many contemporaries (including, for example, Soane), that he was a uniquely sensitive and involuted soul. As he was to write in 1808 to Isabella Pigot, Mrs Fitzherbert's companion:

> I am a different Animal from any other in the whole Creation ...
> my feelings, my dispositions, ... everything that is me, is in all
> respects different ... to any other Being ... that either is now ... or
> in all probability that ever will exist in the whole Universe.
>
> (Quoted in Dinkel, 1983, p.9)

But although the prince's Chinese interiors clearly satisfied his desire for
distinctiveness, the Chinese style was conspicuously unfashionable by
comparison with the rage for the Egyptian or the Greek (mostly inspired
by Nelson's victorious Nile campaign and the researches of Napoleon's
invading archaeologists), or even the picturesque Gothic. The Chinese
was, frankly, vulgar at this juncture, associated with London's famous
public pleasure-grounds, Vauxhall and Ranelagh. Although it promptly
came back into fashion, that was because the prince had espoused it.
Two explanations for this surprising choice can be advanced. One is
personal: that the style satisfied George's nostalgia for 'the forbidden
masquerades and the festive amusements of his youth' (Dinkel, 1983,
p.30). The other possible explanation is that the dream of enlightened
despotism and secure hierarchy so encoded in eighteenth-century
aristocratic views of the Chinese may have been peculiarly congenial to a
prince now leaning towards Toryism in the troubled aftermath of the
French Revolution. At the exact moment, then, that Napoleon was
playing with images of authority in his efforts to invent himself as
emperor, the prince was also playing with representations of his power.
A sharpened nostalgia for the endangered and perilous splendours of
absolute monarchy could be played with and played out in games of
defiantly extravagant style, sourced from accounts of Lord Macartney's
embassy to the Emperor Ch'ien Lung in 1792, lavishly illustrated by
William Alexander. The effect seems, however, to have been ambiguous
if we are to believe one of the prince's slightly puzzled visitors: 'All is
Chinese, quite overloaded with china of all sorts and of all possible
forms ... the effect is more like a china shop baroquement[3] arranged than
the abode of a Prince' (Lewis, 1865, vol.II, p.490).

In the next section we'll look in more detail at how the illusion of
Chineseness is created in these interiors, and at the evolution of the
prince's Chinese interiors from Enlightenment chinoiserie to a full-blown,
stage-set, Romantic version of the East.

---

[3] 'Baroquement' signifies 'in a Baroque fashion': the commentator means that the
china is piled up in an elaborate, ornate and rather overpowering arrangement, very
different from neoclassical simplicity, symmetry or elegance.

4   'Chinese' on the inside

Our evidence for the evolution of the Pavilion's interiors is largely derived from Augustus Pugin's watercolours of the building's interiors and exteriors, executed for a picture-book commissioned around 1820 by the house-proud prince from his architect John Nash, entitled *Views of the Royal Pavilion*, completed in 1826. On the whole, the Pavilion today has been restored to congruence with the *Views*, to appear as it did in 1823 when the building was finished. Let's now look at the Pavilion room by room, starting with the Octagon Hall, the Entrance Hall and the Long Gallery.

EXERCISE   Return to Video 4, band 2 and to Plates 31.3–31.5 in the Illustrations Book, and take a careful look at the details of these three rooms. I'd like you to make notes in answer to the following questions:

1   What elements of the decoration are specifically Chinese?

2   What other elements of the decoration suggest fantasy architecture?

DISCUSSION   *The Octagon Hall.* Fashionably restrained in its colour scheme, this octagonal room none the less boasts two Chinese features – the little bells hanging from the ceiling and the central pendant lantern. Less specific is the elaborate **reticulation** of the cove and ceiling, gently suggesting a tent-like structure, a garden pleasure-pavilion.

The Entrance Hall. Chineseness is suggested most strongly by the dragons painted on the back-lit **clerestory** windows (which are, incidentally, echoed by dragons painted discreetly on the panels) and the lanterns at each corner. But, again, this is a restrained room in terms of its colour scheme, and it is strongly neoclassical in its insistence on certain symmetries, most notably in its provision of a false door to match the real door beside the fireplace.

The Long Gallery. In contrast to the preceding rooms, which suggest a style without setting definite expectations, the Long Gallery establishes without equivocation the Chinese theme that will be played out in so many different varieties of scale and feeling elsewhere in the building (Dinkel, 1983, p.78). Chinese features you might have picked out include the hexagonal lanterns, the silk tassels, the motif of bamboo and birds on the wallpaper, the bells lining the **cornice**, the Chinese figures and porcelain, the dragons and the Chinese god of thunder painted on the skylight, and the *faux* bamboo trellises projecting from the walls and ceiling and forming the banister and rails of the cast-iron staircase leading to the first floor. More nebulously, the colour scheme and the level of decoration are emphatically not neoclassical: the effect is of a riot of daringly clashing colours (pink, blue and scarlet, for example) and intricate geometric multicoloured decoration.

Much less Chinese, but certainly conducing to a fantasy effect, is the startling multiplication of cleverly placed mirrors in **enfilade** to produce a series of special effects. At four points along the corridor large opposing glasses create transverse vistas; in each recess a mirrored niche reflects a tall china pagoda where the lines of sight from one of the drawing rooms and from the corridor meet; and at the ends, where the corridor leads into the Music and Banqueting Rooms, double-doors entirely faced in mirror glass give a perspective of infinite repetition (Dinkel, 1983, p.81). (Contemporaries invariably remarked on the dazzling effect of the mirrors, and further evidence for the effect of the enfiladed mirrors in the Long Gallery is provided indirectly by the account of Soane's use of such mirrors in his country house, Pitzhanger Manor: he too thought they gave 'magical effects', but one of his guests did indeed mistake them for a corridor and was injured so badly that Soane felt obliged to have some of them removed to reduce the illusion – see Batey, 1995, p.23.)

One feature by which you may have been puzzled is the decoration along the cornice in the Entrance Hall, and indeed in the Banqueting Room Gallery, which is related (in miniature) to **fan-vaulting**. This owes more to the other contemporary fantasy style of Gothick than to those associated with the East. Put very briefly, Gothick simply sought to evoke (not very conscientiously) medieval church architecture, pretty much that of the so-called **Perpendicular** period of the first half of the fourteenth century. **Strawberry Hill Gothick**, so named after the home of Horace Walpole (1717–97), is especially lacy and fanciful, as you can see from the example in Figure 31.9.

So far, then, our tour of the Pavilion has identified three styles in use: the neoclassical (which dictates the symmetries of the rooms and their arrangements), the Gothick (which surfaces from time to time) and the Chinese. As we move into the main rooms, however, you should notice another set of references creeping in. We'll start by exploring the rest of the Pavilion, walking into the Music Room Gallery, the Saloon and the Banqueting Room, all originally used as drawing rooms – that is to say, the rooms to which the ladies withdrew to leave the men to drink their port, for coffee and liqueurs, for playing cards after dinner, and for occasional dancing, small concerts and recitals.

EXERCISE   Return to Video 4, band 2, and continue your virtual tour (skip the Banqueting Room for now) to the Music Room Gallery, the Saloon and the Banqueting Room Gallery. By now your eye will be familiar, I hope, with the neoclassical, the Gothick and the Chinese, and you will have

Figure 31.9   Anonymous, The Gallery at Strawberry Hill, *engraving, from Horace Walpole,* A Description of the Villa of Mr H. Walpole at Strawberry Hill, *1784, British Library, London. Photo: by permission of the British Library, London (shelfmark 192.C.16).*

noted, for example, the Chinese **fretwork**, the neoclassical scheme of white and gilding characteristic of earlier interiors by the celebrated architect Robert Adam, and the cornice of tiny Gothick fan vaults. What other influence or influences might be at play here? (Clue: the decorative features that interest me here are principally the pillars in the Music and Banqueting Room Galleries and the tops of the mirrors in the Saloon.)

DISCUSSION   The pillars in the Banqueting Room Gallery are unmistakably meant to look like palm trees (which did not carry Chinese associations), and although the tops of the pillars in the Music Room Gallery look like the sort of Chinese umbrellas carried over high officials in imperial China, snakes rather than dragons curl round the columns. In the Saloon, the tops of the mirrors are unmistakably **Mogul**-inspired in their swelling forms. The mantelpiece and door-frames boast more snakes. There is, in short, a whiff of India about these three rooms, blended with the Chinese fantasy. (If you are especially sharp-eyed, you might also have noticed a faint flavour of the Egyptian in the furniture, especially in the shape of the river-boat couch with crocodile feet.)

The Saloon is, of course, where we started looking at the neoclassical Adamesque scheme portrayed in Rowlandson's sketch of *c*.1789; it is the inside of Holland's rotunda. By 1815 it had metamorphosed, courtesy of Crace, into a Chinese fantasy of a garden arbour, complete with a colourful trellis cornice hung with pendants, panels of Chinese wallpaper and Chinese lanterns. In 1823 Robert Jones swept all of this away in favour of sumptuous crimson, white and gold with an Indian edge. (In its present state it is not quite restored to the Jones scheme, so you should glance again at Plate 31.9 in the Illustrations Book.) In evoking India, the Saloon spoke of empires, both Mogul and British, and as such is perhaps the key to the whole show.

What our investigation suggests is that the Pavilion increasingly displayed an eclectic confederation of styles: neoclassical, Gothick, Chinese and Indian. Some of the original furniture seems also to have had a distinctively Egyptian flavour. Contemporaries would not have been bothered or surprised by this.

EXERCISE Turn to the extract from Maria Edgeworth's novel *The Absentee* (1812) (Anthology II, pp.348–55). The first part of this passage depicts an interview between an interior designer, Mr Soho, and a prospective client, Lady Clonbrony, a would-be social climber over from Ireland. They are discussing new decorations for the gala party which Lady Clonbrony fondly hopes will launch her as a leader of London society. Make a list of some of the more exotic styles Mr Soho is trying to sell.

DISCUSSION I have noted down that Mr Soho recommends furniture and hangings apparently inspired by a fantasy of the Middle East: 'Turkish tent drapery', 'seraglio ottomans' and other 'Oriental' furniture, 'Alhambra hangings' (which feature a dome), and 'Trebisond trellice' wallpaper. He also recommends 'Egyptian hieroglyphic [wall]paper' with an 'ibis border' which had at the time quite different connotations – of Napoleon's archaeological expeditions. He suggests too a 'Chinese pagoda'. These recommendations, combined with the profusion of mythical and exotic animals and birds which he mentions as possible adornments (chimeras, griffins, cranes, sphinxes, phoenixes), make it clear that the Pavilion's fantasy world was more mainstream in temper than perhaps it looks nowadays – albeit much more expensive than Lady Clonbrony's temporary decor.

Edgeworth's Lady Clonbrony was destined for social mortification despite laying out her money on *both* the Turkish tent and the Chinese pagoda, but the association of these extreme styles with entertaining and with the display of a virtuoso and promiscuously exotic taste designed to secure social status is very much what the Pavilion was about.

We have now traversed the whole of Holland's Marine Pavilion, and before we turn our attention to Nash's extensions – the two extraordinary rooms that open from either end of the Long Gallery, the Banqueting Room (interior decoration by Robert Jones) and the Music Room (interior designed by Frederick Crace) – we need to catch up on the prince's projects for massive extension to his holiday home which began to gather speed in 1815.

5   'Indian' on the outside

In 1801 and 1805, first Holland and then his assistant William Porden (1775–1822) had been commissioned to make sketches for altering the exterior to a Chinese style so as to match the extravagantly Chinese interiors, but these projects remained unfulfilled (Plate 31.14 in the Illustrations Book). Drawing on the pictorial records brought back by William Alexander from Lord Macartney's embassy in 1792, Holland and Porden had attempted to invent a Chinese taste in English domestic exteriors, but instead the prince was seized with a new enthusiasm for the Indian – or, to be more precise, the Mogul (rather than the Hindu).

His first foray in this style concerned the stables, built between 1803 and 1808, which housed some 60 horses and dwarfed the Pavilion itself. Although Soane's master, George Dance, had designed the London Guildhall in 1788 in a subtle blend of Islamic and Gothick forms, with the Islamic deriving from illustrations of the Taj Mahal, the immediate inspiration for the prince's stables seems to have come, via Porden's acquaintance with a man called Samuel Pepys Cockerell, from the brothers William and Thomas Daniell, who in 1795 began publishing a series of volumes of sketches entitled *Oriental Scenery* (for an example, see Plate 31.15 in the Illustrations Book). This best-selling work included many aquatints of Delhi, and inspired Cockerell's designs for the new house that his brother, Sir Charles Cockerell, newly back from India and flush with what was slangily referred to as 'nabob' wealth, commissioned him to design at Sezincote in Gloucestershire.

Sezincote is near Moreton-in-Marsh. Although entirely neoclassical in its interior decor, its exterior and its garden are the products of a scholarly eyewitness interest in the civilization of India (see Dinkel, 1983, p.40). Contemporary European interest in India was quite different in kind from the eighteenth-century interest in things Chinese, for it was consciously scholarly and intellectual. In Germany, for example, Goethe read Sir Charles Wilkins's translation of the *Bhagavad-gita* (1795). In Britain intellectuals as politically diverse as the Poet Laureate Robert Southey and the radical atheist Percy Bysshe Shelley were taking their cue from the scholar Sir William Jones's important and arcane translations of Hindu religious poetry, and the translations of Sanskrit literature and philosophy encouraged by the imperialist Warren Hastings. Southey's poem *The Curse of Kehama* (1810) and Shelley's *The Revolt of Islam* (1818), each complete with a vast apparatus of scholarly footnotes on Hindu and Muslim religious observances, respectively, were jostling each other on the shelves of the booksellers. The 'Indian' style was therefore a *recherché*, even an austere, though noble and sublime, style to adopt. The style had other connotations too. It was inevitably and increasingly associated with Britain's rapidly growing military and trading empire. New British interest in Indian culture came back with the nabob wealth of the East India Company and the many scholars and travellers associated with it. The events of 1803, when the British finally occupied Delhi, prompted an explosion of interest in the imperial romance that the subcontinent promised.

Sezincote House drew very precisely from the styles of 'Mogul', as you can see if you compare the engravings of the Jami'Masjid and Sezincote House (Plate 31.15 in the Illustrations Book and Figure 31.10 here). As you can see in more detail from Plates 31.16 and 31.17 (photographs of the house), Sezincote is still fundamentally a neoclassical building in its symmetrical façade of balancing windows and bays, and although you can't see this from these photographs, it is set in a conventionally eighteenth-century fashion so as to dominate its wide sweeping grounds. If the ground-plan is still neoclassical, however, the rotunda has metamorphosed into a Mogul dome; the **parapet** has sprouted mini-**minarets**; the arches of the windows, hooded and recessed, have broken out into scallops and flirt upwards into little bunches of plumes or palms; and the squared-off columns flanking the front door are rather definitely neither Roman nor Greek. The gardens, on the other hand, are conspicuously Hindu in inspiration. Down the side of the house runs a small brook which has been converted into a picturesque garden originally designed by the leading landscape improver Humphrey Repton (Figure 31.11 here and Plate 31.18 in the Illustrations Book). As you will remember from your study of the picturesque in your work on the Lake District, this landscape aesthetic privileges the irregular, the interrupted, the varied and the rough in texture; here, it is heightened by an admixture of the exotic. At the head of the valley there is a carefully reconstructed Hindu temple occupied by a statue of the Hindu sun-god, Surya, looking down over a lotus-shaped temple pool. The stream winds down, under a bridge complete with Brahmin sacred bulls, into the serpent pool which boasts a three-headed serpent spitting a fountain of water (along with the lotus, the serpent was a symbol of regeneration), strongly reminiscent of the serpents winding round the columns in the Music Room Gallery. The 'Hindoo' temple is characteristically stepped and squared off, its silhouette very different from that of the Mogul dome and minarets. The garden has a definite flavour of a wish to be Coleridge's

... deep romantic chasm which slanted
Down the green hill a cedarn cover!
A savage place! as holy and inchanted
As e'er beneath a waning moon was haunted
By woman wailing for her demon-lover!

(Anthology II, p.359)

Figure 31.10   John Martin, Sezincote, *1817, aquatint drawn and etched. Photo: courtesy of the Royal Pavilion, Libraries and Museums, Brighton and Hove.*

Figure 31.11   John Martin, Sezincote, Gloucestershire: The Temple Pool, *1817, print, British Museum, London. Photo: by courtesy of The Trustees of the British Museum.*

But Coleridge's poem was known at this time only to a few intimates. After visiting Sezincote, the prince, as alive as his niece Queen Victoria would be half a century later to the romance of empire, with himself at the centre of the dramatic spectacular, summoned Repton to design something in the same style. Repton's enthusiasm had only been whetted by his designs for the Sezincote gardens; he had become persuaded that architecture and gardening were 'on the eve of some great future change ... in consequence of our having lately become acquainted with the scenery and buildings of India' (quoted in Summerson, 1980, p.103). Again in the Mogul style, Repton's designs were ready in 1806 and published in 1808, but were never executed because the prince's finances were at breaking point. The actual building of the exterior of the Pavilion as we see it today was left in the event to John Nash, who would work in part from Repton's designs. Nash began work on the designs in 1815, and the Pavilion was completed in 1823.

Before we look in some detail at Nash's designs, we need to pause to consider the question of what Mogul architecture might have meant to the prince and his contemporaries, as opposed to Hindu styles. The happy congruence of Mogul and Hindu at Sezincote, which found itself reflected in the indiscriminate way that contemporaries would occasionally refer to the architecture of the Pavilion as 'Hindoo', was not uncontested. This was for a variety of reasons – aesthetic, religious and political. Aesthetically, Mogul architecture was more congenial to Regency fantastic architecture because it had definite affinities with the other main fantasy mode we've already touched upon, the Gothick. You can see this from Plate 31.19 in the Illustrations Book, a photograph of the Regency wing added in Gothick style to Lacock Abbey in Wiltshire. The lacy effect here could just as well be given another twist to become Indian, while the medieval pinnacles could easily metamorphose into minarets, given a little more latitude. As for the religious perspective, Islam, unlike Hinduism, was monotheistic rather than polytheistic, and this seems to have sat better with western cultural expectations at the time. Besides, Hinduism was increasingly being associated in Britain with the practice of *suttee*, the self-immolation of a widow on her dead husband's funeral pyre, dramatized for example in the opening of Southey's poem *The Curse of Kehama*. So much outrage did this provoke in Britain that it would eventually become a moral impetus for the outright take-over of political power in India. Politically, the Moguls (unlike the Hindus) were also associated with fabulously successful empire-building of the sort that the British now aspired to, and with a model of government that contemporaries typically referred to (generally critically) as 'Oriental despotism'. Now Regent as a result of his father's incapacitating illness, the prince seems to have wished to dramatize his increased importance – indeed, it seems to be true that he felt it was part of his role to dramatize national and imperial glory and status both in his person and in his palaces. Certainly, when he became king he was to commission Nash to build him a series of buildings in London that were conspicuously national and imperial in flavour, including Marble Arch. In these years as Regent, his native extravagance was now licensed by his status as monarch in all but name, and he promptly began to play out his own vision of himself as an absolutist *ancien régime* prince in architectural terms. The Pavilion, newly conceived by Nash, was in effect to give him the character of an Oriental potentate; in this context 'Eastern magnificence ... stood for the assertion of monarchical privileges ... in a time of revolution, political, intellectual, and economic' (Dinkel, 1983, p.48).

Turning to Nash's designs, let's compare the Pavilion's façades with those of Sezincote.

EXERCISE   Look again at the illustrations of Sezincote (Figures 31.10–31.11 here and Plates 31.16–31.17 in the Illustrations Book) and then at those of Nash's designs for the exterior of the Royal Pavilion (Plates 31.1–31.2). You may also want to revisit Video 4, band 2 for the detail of the Pavilion's exteriors. Make a list of similarities and differences.

DISCUSSION   *Similarities.* Clearly, Sezincote and the Pavilion both make use of the form of the onion dome topped with a spike. They also share an interest in the style of a minaret, with its mini-dome and smaller spike as accenting features. The same battlemented effect along the edge of the roof (a variant on the standard Georgian parapet) is apparent too. Moreover, a significant number of the windows of both the Pavilion and Sezincote are arched and decorated with scalloping. The lacy effect of the railings at Sezincote also finds an echo in the stone lace-work shading the veranda of the Pavilion's east front. Finally, the squared-off columns of Sezincote are reworked in the many squared-off columns of the Pavilion.

Differences. The overall effect, however, is very different, isn't it? Of course, the Pavilion is larger, which makes some difference, but the real aesthetic contrast is that the design of the Pavilion values profusion. In place of one dome we have ten of varying but much larger sizes; in place of four modest minarets we have ten, much taller and more prominent. Where Sezincote lies quite squat and four-square, evidently a neoclassical design with the Mogul superimposed, the Pavilion, thrusting upwards with strong verticals, is conceived as upwardly mobile (you may also wish to refer to Plate 31.20 in the Illustrations Book, a cross-section through the Pavilion). The Pavilion has also broken out into two tent-like structures, which don't seem to have anything to do with Mogul architecture, although they hint at desert romance. Thus, if one building advertises solid wealth (and admits where it came from), the other breathes fantasy; if one displays a fastidiously scholarly taste indulged among conventional landed proprieties, the other is a wild set of variations upon a theme. One is arguably 'Indian', but the other is visibly

invested in a fantasy of 'the Orient'. Indeed, Nash's unpublished preface
to his *Views of the Royal Pavilion* remarks that the primary aim of prince
and architect was to achieve an effect 'not pedantic but picturesque'
(quoted in Batey, 1995, p.68).

---

6   The Pavilion and the picturesque

Nash's evocation of the picturesque as an aesthetic to describe the
projected exterior for the Pavilion is striking. If neoclassical Palladian
houses had stood four-square in the landscape, rising up out of extensive
lawns and commanding an elaborately naturalistic landscape of grazing
sheep and cattle to the horizon diversified by an ornamental lake, the
picturesque house was instead enfolded within and extended by its
garden. Repton and Nash, in partnership from 1796 to 1802, were two of
the most important exponents of picturesque garden design, deriving
their practice from their personal association with the two theorists of the
picturesque, Uvedale Price and his friend Richard Payne Knight (whom
you have already met in Block 4, Units 16 and 17 on the Lake District).
The picturesque garden was characterized by sinuous shrubberies,
flowerbeds, trellis-work and ornate garden seats, conservatories, flower
corridors and trellised verandas (see Batey, 1995, p.5). The informality of
serpentine winding paths and asymmetrical beds was typically
punctuated by small buildings in various fantasy architectural styles
ranging through the classical, the Gothick, the rustic, the Chinese and so
on. (The house and grounds of Blenheim Palace in Oxfordshire provide
an excellent example of an early eighteenth-century landscape
'improved' by Capability Brown; Luscombe Castle in Devon, by contrast,
is an excellent example of the picturesque style.) The charming
connotations of dream, escape and fantasy that had characterized the
garden follies which dotted the Rococo garden earlier in the eighteenth
century had grown to magnificent size in the Pavilion itself.

Nor was this picturesque aesthetic confined to the exterior of the Pavilion
and its setting; it also conditioned some of the feel of its interiors. In
Repton's and Nash's time, the immediate garden became thought of as an
extension to the house. Interiors broke out into trellised and flowered
wallpaper, and flowed out into conservatories; Edgeworth's *The Absentee*
describes Lady Clonbrony's supper-room decorated with trellised paper
(see Anthology II, p.351). Sir John Soane himself decorated Pitzhanger
Manor with trellis-work and flower sprays. London-based party
entrepreneurs would undertake to expand this aesthetic, tenting and
illuminating their clients' gardens, and filling such marquees with draped
muslin, vast mirrors and huge flower arrangements (Batey, 1995, p.23).
In particular, four elements of the Pavilion's interior might point the way

towards thinking of it as an exercise in translating garden aesthetics into an interior:

1   *The characteristic confusion of inside/outside.* It could, after all, be said that the Pavilion both was inspired by the idea of the sort of temporary party structure in the garden erected by Nash himself for the prince's Carlton House fête in honour of Waterloo, and took the place of such a structure. It was a permanent marquee created especially for parties. The prevalence of ceilings painted to look like skies – as in the Saloon and later the Banqueting Room – and of wallpaper designed to look like trellised veranda or garden pavilion underscores this.

2   *The strong element of fantasy.* While there were fantasy interiors (perhaps most notably in the Strawberry Hill Gothick mode), this sort of fantasy has a much more robust history in garden design, including a proliferation of Chinese garden temples and pavilions in the gardens of the wealthy across the eighteenth and early nineteenth centuries.

3   *Its investment in restless, sauntering admiration.* This interior is designed as a form of entertainment in itself, and is to be appreciated by walking around the house (rather than, say, sitting down in one place).

4   *Its interest in how the figures of guests interacted with the 'landscape'.* In the Rococo garden and the great landscape gardens, the guests were expected both to delight in and admire the landscape, and to figure in it to give it scale and to inhabit its scenario. Thus Horace Walpole on visiting the great landscape garden of Stourhead in Wiltshire, embellished with classical temples, rustic hermitage and grotto complete with river god, found himself rather to his disgust embarking in a boat upon the lake for a thoroughly damp English picnic, really because the genre of the garden demanded it. Equally, one of the more notable effects of exotic architecture and furniture was the way they demanded certain stock responses of astonishment, admiration and delight, at the same time incorporating guests into their own fantasy. These reactions are gratifyingly expressed by one of Lady Clonbrony's guests at her gala:

> The opening of her gala, the display of her splendid reception rooms, the Turkish tent, the Alhambra, the pagoda, formed a proud moment to lady Clonbrony. Much did she enjoy, and much too naturally ... did she show her enjoyment of the surprise excited in some and affected by others on their first entrance.

> One young, very young lady expressed her astonishment so audibly as to attract the notice of all the bystanders. Lady Clonbrony, delighted, seized both her hands, shook them, and laughed heartily; then, as the young lady with her party passed on, her ladyship recovered herself, drew up her head, and said to

the company near her, 'Poor thing! I hope I covered her little *naïveté* properly. How NEW she must be!'

(Anthology II, p.351)

Edgeworth's account of the party goes on to describe the ways in which guests are transformed into props within the overall fantasy provided by the decor:

> Then, with well practised dignity, and half subdued self-complacency of aspect, her ladyship went gliding about – most importantly busy, introducing my lady *this* to the sphynx candelabra, and my lady *that* to the Trebisond trellice; placing some delightfully for the perspective of the Alhambra; establishing others quite to her satisfaction on seraglio ottomans; and honouring others with a seat under the statira canopy.

(Anthology II, p.351)

The guests themselves are to be picturesque, 'dispersed in happy groups, or reposing on seraglio ottomans, drinking lemonade and sherbet – beautiful Fatimas admiring, or being admired' (Anthology II, p.355). The Pavilion furniture similarly insisted upon picturesque Oriental poses. The witty and sophisticated Princess Lieven wrote:

> I do not believe that since the days of Heliogabulus[4] there has been such magnificence and luxury. There is something effeminate in it which is disgusting. One spends the evening half-lying on cushions; the lights are dazzling; there are perfumes, music, liqueurs.

(Quoted in Roberts, 1939, p.110)

As such the Pavilion was itself a sort of extended party game: a stage-set for private theatricals, for a masquerade, for *tableaux vivants*, with a faintly naughty edge. It was an aristocratically exclusive re-creation of the public delights of Vauxhall Gardens, a place haunted by the prince in his wild youth.

7   Experiencing the exotic

So far we have looked in some detail at the interiors of Nash's Pavilion, with the important exception of the Banqueting Room (decorated by Robert Jones) and the Music Room (decorated by Frederick Crace). Both were designed as *coups de théâtre* and it is this aspect of these rooms that I'd like you to focus upon now.

---

[4] This Roman emperor is discussed below, on pp.52–3.

EXERCISE   Return to Video 4, band 2 and look again at the Banqueting Room and the Music Room. You may also wish to look at the contemporary depictions of these two rooms in Plates 31.8 and 31.11 in the Illustrations Book, and to look at the contemporary guidebook descriptions of the rooms given in the AV Notes. Spend a little time practising picking out the Chinese, Indian, Gothick and neoclassical elements which go to making up this Romantic decor, and then make some notes about what effects the rooms achieve and how this is done. Be especially alert to the possibility of 'special effects', such as *trompe l'oeil* and games with perspective.

DISCUSSION   Both rooms, stripped of their decor, turn out to be not at all unlike Soane's neoclassical halls at the Bank of England that you have already looked at in Block 5, Units 22–23. Architecturally, they are both domed square spaces with two lateral extensions, classical in spirit and in principle. That said, however, where Soane's rooms are constructed of real arches and real domes, Nash's arches are not actually supporting anything but are mere wall ornaments in relief. And this tricksy quality is perhaps above all what distinguishes the Romantically improbable style of these rooms from Soane's weightiness and insistence on functionality.

The Banqueting Room. The Oriental magnificence of this room deliberately confounds both chinoiserie (e.g. in the dragons, the wall-paintings, the mini-pagodas sheltering the doors and painted on them) and the Indian (expressed most strongly in the ceiling conceit of the *trompe l'oeil* plantain tree and the lotus glass shades of the huge and dazzling central chandelier). The mixing of the two styles provokes a dramatic conflict between the glamorized violence of the writhing monsters and the sentimental and delicate domesticity of the panels depicting Chinese life.

Jones here achieves a distinctively Regency effect compounded of massive scale and overpowering detail. Entering the Banqueting Room from the Chinese gallery – low-ceilinged and bewilderingly and disorientatingly mirrored – is an astonishing experience. Dreamlike, the scale suddenly expands from the human to the enormous, and the effect is heightened by the apparent glimpse of sky at the apex of the dome. These games of scale also on occasion included miniaturization. The prince briefly brought in the extraordinary talents of Marie-Antoine Carême, the greatest cook of his day, tempted over from France to act as royal chef in the Pavilion's extraordinarily technically advanced kitchens. The confectionery set-pieces for which he was famous were characteristically fantasy buildings in miniature. They included *La ruine de la mosquée turque* (ruin of a Turkish mosque) and *L'hermitage chinois* (Chinese hermitage), made in icing-sugar and set under that astonishing dome. Generally, much of the effect of this room results from the repetition of the same images but on multiple scales: notice, for example, how the lotus and the dragon are repeated.

The Music Room. Again, the scheme for this is late chinoiserie – and as it is designed by Crace it is lighter in feel. Some of the same tricks of scale are also in evidence here in order to astonish guests. These too are centred on the ceiling, which as you will have seen is built up of gilded cockleshells. An effect of greater height was achieved by diminishing the size of the cockleshells towards the apex of the dome, and by changing the tones of the gilding towards the apex. Less obviously, the wall-paintings evoked for contemporaries paintings on Chinese lacquer boxes: the effect was therefore to shrink the spectator within a Chinese miniature grown gigantic. Again, too, the room repeats the same motifs: of serpents, lotus and dragon, varying in scale and prominence, but providing a unifying feeling. The painstaking detailing has a faintly dreamlike effect – fix your eyes on the wallpaper, and sooner or later you are aware that you are looking at a dog-headed serpent, for example. Like the Banqueting Room, the Music Room also intermingles images of extreme violence (manifested in the writhing serpents and dragons) with the domestic or rural idyll, often featuring children. The juxtaposition is more than merely piquant; it introduces a characteristically Romantic tension that we'll come back to below.

We might also remark on some other 'special effects' built into the Pavilion which don't necessarily strike us with the force with which they certainly would have struck contemporaries. The Pavilion was very efficiently and invisibly heated via underfloor heating, an innovation which visitors then found rather stifling. The oil-fired lighting was startlingly profuse, intense and brilliant in an era of candlelight; the thick fitted carpets deadened sound to an unusual extent; the daring and extreme colour harmonies, the many and varied *faux* surfaces, and the use of gas-fired backlighting behind stained-glass panels all heightened the experience, said by one contemporary observer, Mrs Creevey, to be like being inside the Arabian Nights (see the AV Notes). Together with the use of interrupted vista and perspective, of dreamlike repetition and multiplication, of mirrors, of *trompe l'oeil* and of wildly inflated and metamorphic scale, the effect must have been phantasmagoric. With the addition of perfumes and music, the atmosphere was famously heady.

So far I have been concentrating upon the differences between the various rooms in the Pavilion, and upon the differences between the interiors and the exteriors. But although this has been useful for the sake of argument, it is not the whole story. For all that the Comtesse de Boigne was right in her disdainful identification of the styles of the Pavilion as 'heterogeneous', John Evans's remark that the Pavilion's details echoed each other from the smallest to the grandest is equally true (see the AV Notes). Looked at carefully, it becomes clear that all the different room interiors have been designed to echo each other, and to repeat shapes from the exterior too.

EXERCISE   Look once more at the video. Watch it right through and, as you do so, make a list of recurrent motifs and try to sketch repeated shapes. Don't forget that the overall shape may be the same, even if it is reduced, enlarged, inverted, or pretending to be something else (e.g. a bell and a tassel may actually be the same shape, and serve the same function within the decorative scheme, while having different connotations).

DISCUSSION   The easiest thing to do is to make a list of motifs that recur: these include dragons, serpents, bamboo, sunflowers, stars, bells and tassels. It is more difficult to identify the shapes. My list includes:

- what I shall inelegantly call 'bobbles' (which line the parapet on the exterior and the chandeliers in the Music Room, to take two examples);

- bell shapes which, when inverted, turn into flower shapes, or, when multiplied, become pagodas;

- curves flouncing round the Moorish windows and repeated on the cornice of the Entrance Hall and round the mirrors in the Saloon;

- fretwork of every sort;

- leaves growing both up and down (compare the base of the columns on the exterior, the leaves crowning the **cupolas** and the leaves on the plantain tree in the Banqueting Room, for example);

- spiky star shapes,

- reiterated scallops – as in the Saloon wallpaper and the Music Room dome.

The effect of this 'reiteration with variation' is undoubtedly to amplify the dreamlike sense of impending metamorphosis that the Pavilion achieves – you might note, for example, the effect of the way that acanthus leaves turn into dragon manes in the Banqueting Room.

This repetition of shapes and motifs produces a remarkably unified architectural 'vocabulary' throughout the building, despite the different overall effects that the rooms achieve. You might also have noticed the way that the costumes worn by our actors in the video echo and are at home among those apparently *outré* Regency shapes, combining the upward thrust of feathers (compare the flirting tufts at the top of the exterior windows on Sezincote House, for example), the long slender drag of the trains flowing away like serpents' tails, and the horizontal lines of the bodices that double the severities of the Chinese-style fretwork. The costumes look so at home because, idiosyncratic though the Pavilion certainly is and aspired to be, it is grounded within a definite and recognizable Regency aesthetic. George Cruikshank's satiric print *The Beauties of Brighton* (see Plate 31.21 in the Illustrations Book) makes this point too, though the clothes are from a slightly later year, 1826. Indeed, the artist has a lot of fun with pointing up parallels such as the tails of the gentleman's coat which reiterate the tent-like structure on the Pavilion, the top hats echoed in the minarets, and the puffy skirts and sleeves that suggest the domes. The Pavilion, this suggests, was paradoxically both exotic *and* mainstream in its aesthetic.

8   How 'Romantic' is the Pavilion?

At first glance the Pavilion's exoticism might seem to have a good deal to do with contemporary Romantic writers' fascination with the Oriental and exotic. A widespread public interest in these modes put Byron's 'Oriental tales' and Thomas Moore's romance *Lalla Rookh* at the top of the best-seller lists. Coleridge's 'Kubla Khan', after all, is often regarded as the paradigmatic Romantic short poem. So, flouting the conventions of historians of architecture, who designate this period simply as 'Regency', in this section we're going to pursue the relations between the Romantic exotic as expressed in literature and the Pavilion in its final state.

Our investigation so far of the building's effects might already suggest some points of comparison.

EXERCISE   Make a list of some ideas and aesthetic effects that you would consider to be Romantic. (This is a way of looking back across your study to date, and should take you some time – it is *not* easy!) Then see if you can identify any of those ideas and aesthetic effects realized in the Pavilion.

DISCUSSION   Some of the principal tendencies that your study has identified as being Romantic include:

- The abandonment of Enlightenment ideals of knowability and reason, politeness and social responsibility, typically expressed in the neoclassical aesthetic.

- The increasing emphasis put on the unknowable and irrational, and, associated with that, an interest in dreams and fantasies, the development of certain stylistic features (notably the grotesque, the ruined and the fragmentary), and an interest in the sublime.

- An assertion of the primacy of individual imagination and autobiography, and, connected with that, the cult of the strong individual (e.g. Napoleon as well as the Napoleonic-style celebrity of Byron), often associated with Romantic alienation and melancholy.

Some of these tendencies can, I think, be identified within the Pavilion. Its decor is quite strongly interested in producing dreamlike illusions. Just to remind you, these include jolts in scale and proportion, disorientating self-replicating corridors, unnerving shifts between place, obsessive repetition of motifs, the proliferation of the grotesque and the monstrous, and a general ambition to achieve the sensory overload typical of the sublime. These effects are ultimately designed as the intensely personal theatre of an individual imagination.

With this in mind, let's turn to Thomas Moore's *Lalla Rookh*. Moore, as you will remember, was a member of the prince's circle and an enthusiastic admirer of the decorative illusions at the Carlton House ball. He was an Irishman, the friend and biographer of Byron, and *Lalla Rookh* was his first long poem to make a hit. Expensively printed and (supposedly) intensively researched, it was extremely successful both as a poem and in the shape of numerous adaptations, including a lyrical, an equestrian and a spectacular drama, an opera, and a series of lavishly costumed *tableaux vivants* in the Royal Palace of Berlin in 1822 staged to celebrate the visit of the Russian Grand Duke Nicholas (later Tsar Nicholas I).

The frame narrative concerns the journey of an Indian princess to meet her future husband in Shalimar, beguiled by tales told by the handsome young poet Feramorz, in the fashion of the Arabian Nights. Deeply in love with the ineligible poet, the princess seems to be heading for tragedy. All ends happily, however, as the poet casts off his disguise and appears as the caliph himself. There are four inset tales in all: 'The Veiled Prophet of Korassan', 'Paradise and the Peri', 'The Fire-Worshippers' and 'The Light of the Haram'. Passion, sin, forbidden secret loves, suffering and yearning, mystery and disguise, vengeance, romantic death, fabulous feasts and Oriental interiors and exteriors combine to produce charmingly picturesque entertainments, themselves occasions for witty conversations between princess and poet. Given Moore's connections with the prince (of whom he was a frequent guest), it perhaps isn't surprising that *Lalla Rookh* should belong to the same exotic fantasy world embodied in the Pavilion itself. In particular, Moore's poetry is studded with depictions of 'vast illuminated halls', 'glittering Saloons', 'enamell'd cupolas', vistas 'sparkling with the play of countless lamps', minarets, pagodas, grottoes, hermitages and voluptuous enchanted palaces, eclectically set in the Far East and the Middle East. The spirit of Moore's best-seller seems very like the Pavilion: both are unashamedly and explicitly invested in aristocratic entertainment and sexual gratification enjoyed in fabulous and artificial settings. Here, for example, is part of the prose frame narrative describing the wedding party's arrival in camp:

> On their arrival, next night, at the place of encampment, they
> were surprised and delighted to find the groves all round
> illuminated; some artists of Yamtchem having been sent on
> previously for the purpose. On each side of the green alley,
> which led to the Royal Pavilion, artificial sceneries of bamboo-
> work were erected, representing arches, minarets, and towers,
> from which hung thousands of silken lanterns, painted by the
> most delicate pencils of Canton. – Nothing could be more
> beautiful than the leaves of the mango-trees and acacias, shining
> in the light of the bamboo scenery, which shed a light round as
> soft as that of the nights of Peristan.

(Moore, 1879, p.229)

Like the poem, the Pavilion too could be said to be structured as a series
of inset narratives – each room a different elaboration upon a theme, and
each, like each story, designed as a form of seduction. And, like the
Pavilion, the poem is consciously 'heterodox', 'frivolous', 'inharmonious'
and 'nonsensical', as the disapproving comic Vizier Fadladeen remarks in
his capacity as self-appointed literary critic (Moore, 1879, p.301). Above
all, this is a pleasure-palace of a poem, dedicated to the endless renewal
of delight and love:

> Come hither, come hither – by night and by day,
> We linger in pleasures that never are gone;
> Like the waves of the summer, as one dies away,
> Another as sweet and as shining comes on.
> And the love that is o'er, in expiring, gives birth
> To a new one as warm, as unequall'd in bliss;
> And oh! if there is an elysium on earth
> It is this, it is this.

(Moore, 1879, p.299)

For another, very different literary sidelight to illuminate the 'feel' of the
Pavilion in its final state, we're going to turn to a friend and sometime
protégé of William Wordsworth, Thomas De Quincey (1785–1859),
whose fame for us rests principally on a remarkable prose work entitled
The Confessions of an English Opium-Eater (1821–2). In part, this is a
diary recording dreams had under the influence of opium 'in a solid and
a liquid shape, both boiled and unboiled, both East India and Turkey'
(Lindop, 2000, p.58). It is at one dream in particular that we're going to
look, a dream about the Orient which provided the literal source of De
Quincey's narcotics.

EXERCISE   Turn to the extract from De Quincey's *Confessions of an English Opium-
Eater* (Anthology II, pp.355–7). It is written as a diary entry for May 1818.
Compare and contrast De Quincey's vision of the Orient with Moore's.

DISCUSSION   If Moore's vision of the East is of endlessly picturesque, even Rococo, aristocratic pleasures, De Quincey views Asia with horror. In fact, he describes that continent in ways that you might recognize from your study of the sublime in Block 4, Unit 16: he uses the words 'fearful', 'mad', 'horror', 'awful' (in the sense of 'filling us with awe'), 'impressive', 'overpowers', 'sublimity' and 'terror'. He analyses his dream experience in part in terms of a Romantic theory of aesthetics.

This dream-sublime seems to flow largely from an anxiety about *scale*. First, Asia is frighteningly old (as 'the cradle of the human race' it has a superfluity of history). Such age gives rise to elaboration (the religions especially are 'ancient, monumental, cruel, and elaborate' – and, it might be remarked, many), and to the privileging of 'race and name' and *caste* over individual identity. Second, Asia is too large and too full of people, 'swarming with human life'. Added to these problems of scale are those of unnegotiable *difference* and unrecognizability from a European standpoint.

Like Edgeworth's social satire, like Moore's poem and like the Pavilion itself, De Quincey's evocation of a dream experience productively confounds one part of the East with another: a dream China slides into the 'tropical heat and vertical sun-lights' of India, swallowing up Egypt for good measure. Setting aside for a moment the evocation of guilt, punishment, flight and incarceration that De Quincey's prose achieves, I am struck by how elaborately architectural and thoroughly *furnished* this dream is with its confederation of styles: both Lady Clonbrony's party decorations and the Pavilion seem to lie like shadows behind this fantasy. Here are the pagodas, the sphinxes, the crocodiles, the ibises, the snakes, the Chinese houses with cane tables, and the fantasy animal feet so characteristic of Regency furniture. These nightmare experiences of the exotic are explicitly counterposed to the properly domestic, responsible and filial, in the contrast between the dream and De Quincey's awakening to see his children 'come to show me their coloured shoes, or new frocks, or to let me see them dressed for going out'. This might well remind us of the contrast between the monstrous and the domestic played out in the Banqueting and Music Rooms, but for De Quincey it carries a moral weight quite absent from the Pavilion.

Thinking of the East as a dream of power and powerlessness, De Quincey unknowingly reflects Napoleon's meditations upon the East during his Egyptian campaign:

> In Egypt ... I dreamed all sorts of things, and I saw how all I dreamed might be realized. I created a religion: I pictured myself on the road to Asia, mounted on an elephant, with a turban on my head, and in my hand a new Koran, which I should compose.

(Quoted in Rémusat, 1880, vol.I, p.149)

If Napoleon's fantasy of expanding empire finds an eerie, far-off echo in the prince's interior decor, as a discourse De Quincey's dream also has some similarities with the Pavilion, perhaps especially in its interest in physical disorientation, eclectic profusion and the unexpected expansion and contraction of scale. But where the Pavilion suggests that these games are euphoric – with connotations of escape, holiday and the dreamlike – De Quincey rethinks them as nightmarish and grotesque. The Pavilion's effects are controlled and calculated, where De Quincey's dream reels away out of measure. What the Pavilion lacks (understandably!) is what we might call, bathetically, the sheer discomfort of the Romantic as characteristically expressed in literature and painting. Though the prince ambushed his guests with dragons and serpents that seemed to grow out of the wallpaper, the Pavilion was inescapably and necessarily concerned with the provision of comfort. Holiday houses and evening parties, however sumptuous and however picturesque, are never, if successful, really sublime.

The Pavilion's deficiency in the 'Romantic' was directly addressed by two important essayists, William Hazlitt (1778–1830) and Charles Lamb (1775–1834). Hazlitt begins an essay in 1821 by explicitly counterposing the Romantic to the aesthetic of the Pavilion. He challenges an imaginary writer to 'take ... the Pavilion at Brighton, and make a poetical description of it in prose or verse. We defy him' (see Anthology II, p.361).

EXERCISE   Read the extract from Hazlitt's essay, 'Pope, Lord Byron, and Mr Bowles' (1821) (Anthology II, pp.360–3). Identify Hazlitt's main reasons for insisting that the Pavilion is not poetical in itself, nor a suitable poetic subject.

DISCUSSION   The problem with the Pavilion is to do in part with the relation between 'art' and 'nature'. 'Art', unless ruined, is overly complete and, in the case of the Pavilion, is new, successful, self-sufficient, over-blown, deeply vain. As property, the palace is imbued with the 'practical prosaic idea' of the haves and have-nots; because aristocratic exclusivity is built into it, it excludes 'cordial sympathy' of the sort that builds a community. Hazlitt seems to suggest that by contrast nature (and poetry) acts as something which can be had and enjoyed by all, even those who are not property owners. Poetry, too, can provide that which a building, according to Hazlitt, cannot: emotion, sentiment, and associations of melancholy, dread and decay.

This counterposing of art and nature, and of art and the sublime, is also addressed by Charles Lamb in an essay of 1833 entitled 'On the barrenness of the imaginative faculty in the productions of modern art'.

Lamb amplifies his discussion of contemporary painting with a revealing (and possibly apocryphal) anecdote, sometimes dated to around 1806, about the Pavilion:

> The court historians of the day record, that at the first dinner given by the late King (then Prince Regent) at the Pavilion, the following characteristic frolic was played off. The guests were select and admiring; the banquet profuse and admirable; the lights lustrous and oriental; the eye was perfectly dazzled with the display of plate, among which the great gold salt-cellar, brought from the regalia in the Tower for this especial purpose, itself a tower! stood conspicuous for its magnitude. And now the Rev. * * * * the then admired court Chaplain, was proceeding with the grace, when, at a signal given, the lights were suddenly overcast, and a huge transparency was discovered, in which glittered in golden letters –
>
> 'BRIGHTON – EARTHQUAKE – SWALLOW-UP-ALIVE!'
>
> Imagine the confusion of the guests; the Georges and garters, jewels, bracelets, moulted upon the occasion! The fans dropt, and picked up the next morning by the sly court pages! Mrs. Fitz-what's-her-name fainting, and the Countess of * * * * holding the smelling-bottle, till the good-humoured Prince caused harmony to be restored by calling in fresh candles, and declaring that the whole was nothing but a pantomime *hoax*, got up by the ingenious Mr. Farley, of Covent Garden, from hints which his Royal Highness himself had furnished! Then imagine the infinite applause that followed, the mutual rallyings, the declarations that 'they were not much frightened,' of the assembled galaxy.
>
> (Lamb, 1912, p.259)

What interests me about this anecdote is that the 'pantomime *hoax*' (which reworks the biblical episode of Belshazzar's feast in which a tyrannous Persian king sees a hand writing on the wall a divine prophecy of his own utter downfall) provides in a comedic mode that Romantic drama which Hazlitt has described as being outside the range of the building itself. Here are the terrors of the sublime earthquake, here is the fearful disruption to the gay scene which might perhaps remind you of Byron's evocation of the premature end to the ball at Brussels on the eve of Waterloo (see Block 6, Units 29–30). Sublime nature in the shape of the earthquake, however, turns out to be merely elaborate artifice – a party piece.

If we turn once again, and for the last time, to Coleridge's poem 'Kubla Khan', we can see that Hazlitt's privileging of nature and poetry over architecture and wealth is echoed in it. Without giving a comprehensive reading of this poem, which must be one of the most famous, mystifying and intensively argued-over in the English language, it is possible to say that it takes as its protagonist a man whose name was for contemporaries a byword for oppression and cruelty, whose empire-building was associated by Coleridge with Napoleon's devastation of Europe. Within this poem about the nature of Romantic creativity, the chief preoccupation is the delicate balance of the Khan's astonishing architectural *tour de force* with the forces of nature:

> The shadow of the dome of pleasure
> Floated midway on the waves;
> Where was heard the mingled measure
> From the fountain and the caves.
> It was a miracle of rare device,
> A sunny pleasure-dome with caves of ice!

(Anthology II, p.359)

The whole is a precariously stable confection of art and nature, of the solid dome shadowed on the shifting water, of domed roof and founding caves, of pleasure and privation. This pleasure-palace is, like the Prince Regent's, threatened by ominous rumours and echoes – 'Ancestral voices prophesying war' ('Kubla Khan', l.30). If we focus on the final section of the poem, however, it turns out that the Romantic poet challenges the power of the Khan himself, claiming to have the same power of creativeness through the wonderful and tyrannical power of song to capture the imagination of his audience and to strike them with sublime horror:

> ... with music loud and long,
> I would build that dome in air,
> That sunny dome! those caves of ice!
> And all who heard should see them there,
> And all should cry, Beware! Beware!
> His flashing eyes, his floating hair!

(Anthology II, p.360)

The power of the Romantic artist challenges and replicates the absolute power of the imperial tyrant. The poet faces off the prince, and this, parenthetically, returns us to our discussion in Block 6 of newly emerging Romantic notions of art and the artist.

9   What the world said – or, the politics of the exotic

So far we have mostly been concerned with the making of the Pavilion, treating it as a product of the confluence between the prince's virtuoso taste, his fluctuating reserves of cash and his patronage of the talents of a series of architects and designers, especially John Nash. We have also remarked in passing that the flamboyant idiosyncrasy of the Pavilion seems to be attributable in large part to the prince's nostalgia for absolutism, expressed in an era of constitutional monarchy and seemingly ever-impending revolution. 'Oriental despotism' had had very negative connotations of barbarism and arbitrariness throughout the eighteenth century, but here George seems to have been revaluing it in relation to his own power. Indeed, across Europe the Oriental exotic seems to have been an aesthetic linked by supporters as well as critics to the restoration of hereditary monarchies (this, at any rate, is one possible reading of the court theatricals designed around the dramatization of *Lalla Rookh* in Berlin in 1822). The prince's fantasy of his role as monarch, as we have also remarked, must have been much strengthened by the financial realities of Britain's growing empire in the East. Although we have taken a look at Hazlitt's and Lamb's passing comments, we have not yet extensively considered what everyone else at the time thought about it. To do this is to think about the Pavilion principally as a cultural and political fact within early nineteenth-century British culture.

From very early on the Pavilion was itself an attraction, and by 1809 it appears that it was intermittently open to the polite and paying public. Certainly its interiors were of considerable interest to the public, if we can judge by the blow-by-blow descriptions of them given over many pages in Attree's *Topography of Brighton* (1809). In January 1820 came ticketed admission to the state apartments.

EXERCISE   Turn to the selection of contemporary verdicts upon the Pavilion, organized chronologically, made by insiders and outsiders (Anthology II, pp.364–8). You will also find some pictorial comments in Plates 31.22–31.23 in the Illustrations Book. Study them carefully, and then make some notes about what you can deduce from this evidence about contemporary views of the monarchy.

DISCUSSION   The comments begin to be more disapproving the more *outré* and extravagant the Pavilion becomes both inside and outside. Although John Evans makes a spirited attempt to constitute the prince's whim into something that redounds to the nation's credit, the more general tone is one of moral disapproval of frivolity and self-indulgence, a strong tendency to refuse to admire princely dignity and instead to regard the Pavilion as bizarre and downright unBritish. This is the effect of those insistent comparisons of the domes to turnips, the minarets to extinguishers and the like: they point up how thoroughly non-indigenous and aggressively useless the building was.

Critics had a point. Despite that interesting remark of the prince's to the effect that he chose the Chinese style over traditionally Whiggish

Neoclassicism for fear of being thought 'Jacobinical' (i.e. sympathizing with the French revolutionaries), and despite his shock conversion to his father's political allegiance to Toryism (both actual and imaginative) on taking power in 1811, the Pavilion was very evidently a fancy-dress holiday from those responsible and 'official' styles associated historically either with the aristocracy or with the monarchy. From being a fantasy of escape from his father's authority, it had become an escape from the circumscribed realities of constitutional monarchy. In the teeth of the scandal of George's treatment of his estranged queen, culminating in the (ultimately aborted) divorce proceedings against her in 1820, and more generally in the context of severe agricultural depression, of the post-war slump, and of the great hardship and widespread agitation produced by the Industrial Revolution and the urbanization that came with it, the Pavilion was inflammatory. As 'Humphrey Hedgehog' (the pseudonym of John Agg) was to write in *The Pavilion; or, A Month in Brighton* (1817) not long before the Peterloo riots in Manchester:

> In the midst of the most aggravated public distress, when penury and woe walk the streets hand in hand, and thousands are actually starving, the prodigalities of those great ones of the earth ... present a fair field for satire ... the dazzling and cleansing fire of patriotism has dwindled into the impure and unwholesome flame of self-interest, and every better feeling and principle appear to be entirely merged and lost in the giddy and intoxicating vortex of sensuality.

(Hedgehog, 1817, vol.I, pp.10–11)

'Hedgehog' does his best to convert his prince through his experiences as 'a Caliph in disguise', bringing him to admit that he 'had in too many instances, preferred private enjoyment to the welfare of the state' and to resolve to do some 'patriotic good' (Hedgehog, 1817, vol.II, pp.174–5, 177). But the Pavilion's insouciance and arrogance, its utter lack of restraint, its dubious flavour, viewed in the context of similar Romantic fantasy narratives invested in the East and its not entirely respectable pleasures, seemed to need a catastrophic ending to provide a properly moral outcome. The Princess Lieven's remarks likening the prince to Heliogabalus, which we've already noted, are equally a stinging critique of the outlandishness of his taste and of the questionable morality of power thus imagined. Heliogabalus, as the educated would have known, was a Roman emperor who, during his brief four-year reign, became notorious for 'inexpressible infamy' including transvestism and homosexuality. In the magisterial words of the historian Edward Gibbon, 'Rome was at length humbled beneath the effeminate luxury of Oriental despotism' (Gibbon, 1998, pp.130, 128). Before he was assassinated, his career as portrayed by Gibbon has a whiff of the Prince Regent's, at least as described by his many critics:

> A capricious prodigality supplied the want of taste and elegance; and, whilst Elagabulus [*sic*] lavished away the treasures of his

people in the wildest extravagance, his own voice and that of his flatterers applauded a spirit and a magnificence unknown to the tameness of his predecessors.

(Gibbon, 1998, p.130)

If judgement overtook both Belshazzar and Heliogabalus in the midst of their sensual excesses, so too did it overcome the villain caliphs of many important contemporary Romantic fantasy narratives. Two will do to make the point – Beckford's novel *Vathek* and Southey's poem *The Curse of Kehama*. In *Vathek*, for example, the cruel sensualist caliph finally makes his way to the subterranean halls of Eblis, where he discovers the worthlessness of the riches and luxuries he has lusted and searched after, and is punished for his sins when his own heart and the hearts of all the damned burst into flames in their living bodies. Southey's equally cruel and part-supernatural Rajah Kehama eventually finds himself under the dominion of the lord of hell. In flat contradiction therefore to the princely complacency of the Pavilion, Orientalist tales, poems and paintings of the period are typically and variously critical of despotism, whether enlightened, Napoleonic or Bourbon. Such is one reading of Delacroix's vast and controversial canvas *The Death of Sardanapalus* (1827–8), derived in part from Byron's drama critical of tyranny, *Sardanapalus* (1821). It is to the consideration of this painting that we turn in the next unit to expand our understanding of Romantic exoticism in fine art.

10   Conclusion

Just before you move on in your studies, however, you should pause to consider what key points you might take away from this unit. Here are some questions for you to chew on to help you do this.

How has your study of the Pavilion changed or elaborated the picture of the period that you have been building up? Does it, for example, suggest that Romanticism was not monolithic, that there were lots of *different* kinds and understandings of what was Romantic, and that some of them might even have been mutually contradictory? Does it suggest that not everyone was living in a 'Romantic' fashion in the so-called Romantic age? Or does it suggest that everyone and everything was subtly altered by what Hazlitt was to call so memorably 'the spirit of the age' so that even the monarchy, that relic of an older age, could fall victim to a Romantically alienated individualism?

If these questions baffle you at this stage, then you are welcome to set them aside, but if they prompt you to look back over this unit before moving on, that will be all to the good!

Appendix: The Royal Pavilion – significant dates

1762   Birth of George Augustus Frederick, Prince of Wales.

1783   First visit to Brighton by the Prince of Wales.

1787   Henry Holland builds the Marine Pavilion.

1795   Prince of Wales marries Caroline, Princess of Brunswick.

1801   Significant extensions made to the Marine Pavilion.

1802   Introduction of the 'Chinese taste' to the interior decorations.

1811   Prince of Wales created Prince Regent.

1815   John Nash's transformation of the Pavilion begins.

1820   Prince Regent succeeds to the throne as George IV.

1822   Completion of the exterior of the Pavilion.

1823   Completion of the interior of the Pavilion.

1827   George IV's last visit to Brighton.

1830   Death of George IV.

References

Attree, H.R. (1809) *Topography of Brighton: and, Picture of the Roads, from Thence to the Metropolis*, Brighton and London.

Austen, J. (1967) *Pride and Prejudice*, in *The Novels of Jane Austen*, ed. R.W. Chapman, vol.2, Oxford, Oxford University Press (this series first published 1923).

Batey, M. (1995) *Regency Gardens*, Princes Risborough, Shire Publications.

Dinkel, J. (1983) *The Royal Pavilion, Brighton*, Brighton, Philip Wilson Publishers and Summerfield Press.

Fisher, F.G. (1800) *Description of Brighthelmstone, and the Adjacent Country; or, the New Guide for Ladies and Gentlemen Visiting that Place of Health and Amusement*, Brighthelmstone (Brighton).

Gibbon, E. (1998) *The Decline and Fall of the Roman Empire: 28 Selected Chapters*, ed. A. Lentin and B. Norman, Ware, Wordsworth Classics.

Hazlitt, W. (1933) 'Pope, Byron, and Mr Bowles', in *The Works of William Hazlitt*, ed. P.P. Howe, 21 vols, London and Toronto, Dent, vol.19 (this essay first published 1821).

Hedgehog, H. [John Agg] (1817) *The Pavilion; or, A Month in Brighton: A Satirical Novel*, 2 vols, London.

Hibbert, C. (1973) *George IV*, Harmondsworth, Penguin.

Lamb, C. (1912) 'On the barrenness of the imaginative faculty in the productions of modern art', in *Elia and the Last Essays of Elia*, ed. E.V. Lucas, London, Methuen (first published 1833).

Leslie, C.R. (1951) *Memoirs of the Life of John Constable Composed Chiefly of his Letters*, London, Phaidon Press (first published 1843).

Lewis, T. (ed.) (1865) *Extracts of the Journals and Correspondence of Miss Berry from the Year 1783 to 1852*, 3 vols, London, Longman, Green and Co.

Lindop, G. (ed.) (2000) *Works of Thomas De Quincey*, 18 vols, vol.2: *Confessions of an English Opium-Eater 1821–2*, London, Pickering and Chatto.

Lloyd, M. (1809) *Brighton: A Poem. Descriptive of the Place and Parts Adjacent ...*, London.

Moore, T. (1879) *The Poetical Works of Thomas Moore*, ed. C. Kent, London, George Routledge and Sons.

Pasquin, A. [pseudonym] (1796) *The New Brighton Guide: Involving a Complete, Authentic and Honorable Solution of the Recent Mysteries of Carlton House; A Moral Epistle from the Pavilion at Brighton to Carlton House, London*, 6th edn, London.

Rémusat, C.E.J. de (1880) *Memoirs*, trans. F.S. Hoey, 2 vols, London, Sampson Lowe.

Roberts, H.D. (1939) *A History of the Royal Pavilion, Brighton*, London, Country Life.

Summerson, J. (1980) *The Life and Work of John Nash Architect*, London, Allen and Unwin.

Temperley, H. (ed.) (1930) *Princess Lieven: Unpublished Diary*, London, Jonathan Cape.

Further reading

Barlow, A. (n.d.) *The Prince and his Pleasures: Satirical Images of George IV and his Circle*, Brighton, The Royal Pavilion, Libraries and Museums.

Dinkel, J. (1983) *The Royal Pavilion, Brighton*, Brighton, Philip Wilson Publishers and Summerfield Press.

Evans, J. (1821) *Recreation for the Young and the Old: An Excursion to Brighton, with an Account of the Royal Pavilion*, Chiswick.

Goff, M. (1976) *The Royal Pavilion, Brighton*, London, Michael Joseph.

Morley, J. (1984) *The Making of the Royal Pavilion Brighton*, London, Philip Wilson for Sothebys.

Murray, V. (1998) *High Society in the Regency Period, 1788–1830*, Harmondsworth, Penguin.

Musgrave, C. (1959) *The Royal Pavilion: An Episode in the Romantic*, London, L. Hill.

Rowlandson, T. and Wigstead, H. (1789) *Excursion to Brighthelmstone in 1789*.

Unit 32
Delacroix: reluctant Romantic?

Prepared for the course team by Linda Walsh

Contents

Study components

Weeks of study	Supplementary material	Audio-visual	Anthologies and set books
1	AV Notes Illustrations Book	Video 4	Anthology II

Objectives

After studying this unit, you should be able to:

- identify those aspects of Delacroix's art that qualify it as 'Romantic';
- come to an understanding of the interplay between classicism and Romanticism in Delacroix's art;
- appreciate the nature of Delacroix's fascination with the Oriental and the exotic even before he visited Morocco.

1   Introduction

Ferdinand-Victor-Eugène Delacroix (1798–1863) was an artist raised amid
the heroism and turmoil of Napoleon's regime but whose artistic career
began in earnest after Waterloo. His father (who died in 1805) held
important administrative, ambassadorial and ministerial posts during both
the Revolution and Napoleon's rule. His brothers had fought for
Napoleon, one being killed heroically in 1807 at the battle of Friedland,
the other a general who was made a baron of the empire before being
retired (as was the custom) on half-pay. As Delacroix's mother had died
in 1814, when he was still fairly young, he was left in the care of an
older sister, who had little time to devote to him and struggled with the
precarious financial position of the family. Delacroix's own (artistic) glory
was to come later and he is often described as part of the 'generation of
1820' (Spitzer, 2001, p.9). This generation, coming of age between 1814
and 1825, had witnessed the disappointed hopes of Napoleonic empire,
and it has been suggested that this sense of loss helped to determine
their Romantic mindset (see Brookner, 2000). Having seen the Old
Regime swept away, they looked on as the monarchy was restored after
Napoleon's defeat. Those who had earlier supported the Revolution now
tried their luck as royalists. Although he quickly gained a reputation as a
rebellious Romantic, Delacroix was always ill at ease with this perception
of him. Like many artists of the Romantic generation, he sought public
recognition. As you will see, his career was to be a constant struggle to
reconcile a radical aesthetic with the demands of public taste and
longstanding, well-respected artistic traditions.

The Oriental and the exotic played a central role in this process of
artistic negotiation and reconciliation. The Enlightenment's preoccupation
with 'exotic' lands as part of an indirect critique of western European
societies increasingly competed with visions of the East as a site of
fantasy, desire and sensuous pleasure. In Unit 31 on the Royal Pavilion at
Brighton, you saw how a taste for Oriental and exotic decoration,
inherited from the eighteenth century, was adapted to a somewhat
decadent expression of power, social status and material consumption.
Like the Prince Regent's Pavilion, Delacroix's work also exemplified in
many respects a specifically Romantic concern with the Oriental and
exotic as a means of unleashing and expressing personal desire. His
interest lay largely in Greece, Turkey and Morocco. In a typical switch
from an enlightened to a Romantic perspective, the psychological and
social ideas opened up by the Enlightenment's consideration of such
places gave way to the application of those ideas to a process of artistic
self-exploration and self-expression. And yet, as we shall see, Delacroix
was not always so clearly on the side of Romanticism. His 1832 journey
to Morocco would be a crucial, transforming influence on his career.

First, it is necessary to establish how Delacroix developed his artistic
thought, values and practice in the early part of his career in order to

appreciate the full impact on his art of a concern with Oriental and exotic subjects. Our starting point will be the painting that caused the greatest furore of the artist's career.

2   *The Death of Sardanapalus*

Plate 32.1 in the Illustrations Book is a reproduction of Delacroix's *The Death of Sardanapalus*, believed to have been completed sometime between November 1827 and January 1828. It draws on a legend, fabricated in the *Persika* by the Greek writer Ksetias (fourth century BCE), that had already featured in a play by Byron entitled *Sardanapalus*, published in 1821. It concerns an Assyrian ruler whose palace was threatened by his rebellious subjects. Sardanapalus, descendant of Semiramis, was the last king of Nineveh, a city roughly halfway between the Mediterranean and the Caspian Sea in present-day Iraq. According to the legend, he died in 876 BCE. In order to avoid the humiliation of defeat by his subjects (a theme that would have evoked, in Delacroix's era, the revolutionary mob), he ordered himself, his palace and all his prized possessions (including his favourite concubine, Myrrha) to be burned and destroyed. In Delacroix's version, unlike Byron's, Sardanapalus meets his fate not just with Myrrha, but with an entire roomful of concubines and slaves. Delacroix probably drew on a number of sources in the visualization of this incident. Apart from Byron, it's thought that he was also influenced by the Greek historian Diodorus (first century CE), the Roman historian Quintus Curtius (also first century CE) and possibly an engraving of a pseudo-Etruscan relief of the incident (see Johnson, 1981, pp.117–18). It has also been suggested (see Lambertson, 2002) that the conception and iconography of Delacroix's painting might have been inspired by similar work by Charles-Émile Champmartin, an artist with whom Delacroix was acquainted. Champmartin had visited the Near East and in 1828 completed a large-scale Oriental massacre scene, *Massacre of the Janissaries* (see Plate 32.2 in the Illustrations Book). However, the uncommissioned *Sardanapalus* was probably, above all, a product of Delacroix's fancy. Archaeological accuracy was certainly not possible as Nineveh had not yet been excavated. The following explanatory text was published in the booklet accompanying the paintings at the 1827–8 Salon, where Delacroix's canvas was exhibited:

> *Death of Sardanapalus.* The rebels besieged him in his palace ... Lying on a superb bed, atop an immense pyre, Sardanapalus orders his eunuchs and palace officers to slit the throats of his women, his pages, and even his horses and favourite dogs; none of the objects that served his pleasure should survive him ... Aïsheh, a Bactrian woman, couldn't bear that a slave should kill her and hung herself from the columns supporting the vault ...

Baleah, Sardanapalus's cupbearer, finally set fire to the pyre and threw himself in.

(Quoted in Johnson, 1981, pp.114–15; trans. Walsh)

Aïsheh is in the centre of the top of the painting; Baleah is in the centre of the painting's right-hand edge, accompanied by a figure holding his hand to his head. He is signalling to Sardanapalus that, as the rebels have gained ground, the order to set fire to the palace has already been given. We can see flames in the background. Sardanapalus himself reclines on his bed, in the top left-hand corner, gazing in Baleah's direction. The diagonal between him and Baleah divides the painting into two sections, each full of incident. To the right of the bed, as Aïsheh hangs herself, a slave is preparing to kill a woman lower down. To the left of the bed, we see a woman carrying poison in a jewel-encrusted jug; other figures kill themselves, are convulsed by fear or lie dying. In the right foreground a nude woman is having her throat slit and in the bottom left-hand corner a black slave is killing a horse.

The painting provoked a furore because both its subject and the manner in which it was painted were felt to be excessive: this delirious orgy, playing on Byronic notions of fieriness (see Block 6, Units 29–30) and Faustian concoctions of creative and destructive energies (see Block 6, Units 26–27), was not what critics and public had come to expect of grand history painting. Its massive size (just under four by five metres) magnified its effect. In fact, the painting had only narrowly been voted into the exhibition by the Salon jury. The following critique, by Étienne-Jean Delécluze, a former pupil of David, was typical:

> M. Delacroix's *Sardanapalus* found favour neither with the public nor with the artists. One tried in vain to get at the thoughts entertained by the painter in composing his work; the intelligence of the viewer could not penetrate the subject, the elements of which are isolated, where the eye cannot find its way within the confusion of lines and colours, where the first rules of art seem to have been deliberately violated. *Sardanapalus* is a mistake on the part of the painter.

(Quoted in Jobert, 1998, p.83)

Most assessments, like this one, slated the painting's lack of compositional logic and its riot of colour. Delacroix was said to be 'hot-headed'; his work had gone 'beyond the bounds of independence and originality'; in the 'delirium of his creation' he had been carried 'beyond all bounds'; 'almost unanimously the spectators find it ridiculous' (from reviews quoted in Jobert, 1998, pp.81–3). The Director of Fine Arts summoned Delacroix in order to tell him that if he wished to receive future government commissions (which were, in any case, relatively rare in restoration France) he would have to alter his style: the government refused to purchase the work. The painting remained unsold until 1846, when it was bought by a banker, John Wilson.

Let's look now at the causes of the widespread antipathy to this painting, a 'mistake' that would motivate Delacroix, in the remainder of his career, to be better understood.

Why were the colour and composition of *Sardanapalus* so controversial?

In order to understand the furore created by *Sardanapalus* it will be helpful to compare the work with others more acceptable to the domain of public art. With this in mind, you are asked here to work on two short exercises designed to explore the radical nature of Delacroix's deathbed scene. In each case, you will be asked to compare images and extract their principal similarities and differences.

EXERCISE   Compare Delacroix's *Sardanapalus* and David's *Andromache mourning Hector* (Plates 32.1 and 32.3 in the Illustrations Book). Make brief comparisons between these paintings, focusing on the general organization of the picture space; the position of the deathbeds and the use of linear perspective (the use of straight lines that appear to recede into the picture space and converge, thus suggesting depth or distance); and the implied position (if any) of the viewer.

DISCUSSION   The space represented by David's painting is intelligible, logical and ordered. There is a clear sense of linear perspective in the receding lines of the floor which lead the viewer's eye into the scene and to an identifiable convergence point or viewer's 'eye level' just above Andromache's head. The elements of the painting relate clearly to one another in scale so that, for example, it is obvious that Andromache is closer to us than the body of Hector, which is, in turn, closer to us than the background colonnade. There is a clear recession into the depth or distance from the viewer, based on an imagined series of vertical planes or layers slicing through the picture space, rather like parallel vertical slots or dividers in an imaginary three-dimensional box. The deathbed is arranged horizontally along one of these planes so that it offers a dignified profile of the dead hero's corpse. The two principal figures stand out clearly from a dark, neutral background and are arranged symmetrically so that the overall composition is balanced.

By contrast, Delacroix's painting offers no clear recession into depth. There is no logical sense of scale or perspective. For example, the woman reclining behind the nude with arching back seems to be too close to her to appear so small. Sardanapalus's head appears diminutive by comparison with those of the foreground figures. Figures and objects are tumbled together in a way that makes it difficult to say with any confidence which are supposed to be closer to the viewer than others. Look, for example, at the foreground figures, who seem to form a frieze – like a 'cut-out' imposed uneasily on the rest of the painting. And finally the floor, far from providing a clear path for the viewer's eye to follow, seems to cave in at the foot of the painting so that it is difficult to imagine how, for example, the rearing horse has entered the scene at all. The deathbed itself is almost propelled, like a magic carpet, from the top left-hand corner, and slices diagonally through the scene without any clear relationship to the angle of the walls around it. There is no easily identifiable point from which to view this scene, which also appears to have been cropped in an unnatural way, as if the real clues to what is going on are out-of-frame. If anything we, as viewers, are suspended above the chasm apparently about to engulf Sardanapalus's rich treasures. Faces are painted as if we see them all from the same height – there is no use of foreshortening – and yet we know this cannot possibly be so, as logic would dictate that we view some chins from below, some heads from above.

All of these disorientating effects of Delacroix's composition were noted by his contemporaries, whose mindset was very much attuned to more legible treatments of picture space. This was exemplified by David, whose approach to painting represents a particularly austere interpretation of the **neoclassical style** established in eighteenth-century French art. It contributed to the political aims of the Revolution and First Empire, was admired and emulated by many artists, and remained influential in the Academy and critical circles of Delacroix's time. It was derived from a restrained, dignified branch of Renaissance classicism, drawing principally on Raphael and popularized in France through the example of artists such as the seventeenth-century master Nicolas Poussin (see Figure 32.1). Later eighteenth-century artists such as Jean-Baptiste Greuze (see Figure 32.2) adapted Poussin's neoclassical deathbed formula (a frieze-like composition structured around straight, horizontal lines and uncluttered spaces), which also found dramatic expression in David's *Death of Socrates* (see Plate 5.2 in the Illustrations Book). Moreover, in 1827, the year in which Delacroix's *Sardanapalus* was being completed, Ingres, by then a famous representative of Neoclassicism, exhibited his *Apotheosis of Homer* (Plate 32.4). Although he was perceived as departing radically from David's approach, he had nevertheless studied under him and was identified as adhering in important ways to the master's neoclassical example.

In many neoclassical paintings there is a clear, logical, **planimetric** structure to the composition: that is, a series of implied horizontal and vertical planes (straight layers or 'slices' through the imagined three-dimensional space of the painting) along which the whole is structured, so that the composition remains taut, stable and balanced. This stability

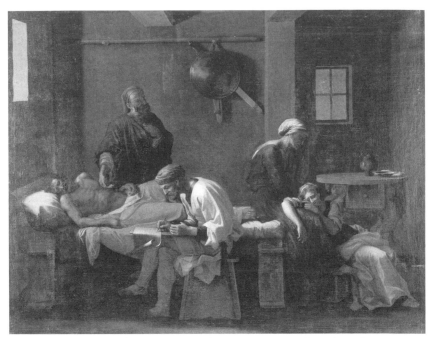

Figure 32.1   Nicolas Poussin, The Testament of Eudamidas, *c.1643–4, oil on canvas, 110.5 x 138.5 cm, Statens Museum for Kunst, Copenhagen. Photo: DOWIC Fotografi.*

Figure 32.2   Jean-Baptiste Greuze, The Wicked Son Punished, *1778, oil on canvas, 130 x 163 cm, Louvre, Paris. Photo: © RMN/ Hervé Lewandowski.*

was often achieved partly through the use of the straight horizontal lines of classical architecture, which locked figures and objects into a geometric 'grid'. Figures, derived from antique statuary, are idealized rather than realistic, and arranged hierarchically so that heroes and protagonists and the planes on which they are located are clearly dominant. Neoclassical compositions of the late eighteenth and early nineteenth centuries express the traditional values of a **classical style**: simplicity, unity, order, idealism, balance, symmetry and a general respect for rules and reason. They also adhere to the traditional classical practice of studying antique statuary and the posed academic model as a basis for figure drawing: if 'nature' was to be 'imitated' this had to be in a highly selective, idealizing and refining way (see Block 6, Units 24–25 on *la belle nature* – beautiful, or idealized, nature). The neoclassical style developed and championed by David offers a particularly striking version of the classical characterized by a stark linearity: clearly delineated, outlined or contoured figures and objects, standing out from a neutral, non-distracting background, and often arranged horizontally so that they line up directly in front of the viewer.

The surface finish of a neoclassical painting is smooth, so that there is no distracting surface 'dazzle' or appeals to the senses of touch and sight that would detract from intellectual impact. Eloquent gesture, designed to assist narrative intelligibility, is also characteristic. In the years preceding the French Revolution, the Neoclassicism introduced by David, with its stripped bare, linear, austere style and republican overtones, had been controversial (see Plate 32.5 in the Illustrations Book, *The Lictors returning to Brutus the Bodies of his Sons*). David's pupils – Girodet, Gérard, Guérin and Ingres – subsequently assisted their master in consolidating the status of Neoclassicism by adapting its potential to the requirements of the Napoleonic empire. Generally, this elevated style became accepted as appropriate to the morally and intellectually elevated history genre favoured (as you saw in Block 2, Unit 9) by the Academy and required for grand, public display. It suited a broad cultural preference for the archetypal and the didactic. By the time Delacroix began his career as a painter, Neoclassicism had lost much of its Davidian radicalism and had become a style with which the Academy was both familiar and comfortable.

Delacroix does not draw on this neoclassical tradition. He uses an alternative deathbed tradition, in which the bed is artificially raised and tilted towards the viewer to allow a fuller view of the dead or dying. See, for example, Ménageot's *Leonardo de Vinci, dying in the Arms of Francis the First* (Figure 32.3) and Rembrandt's etching of *The Death of the Virgin* (Figure 32.4). Delacroix tilts and raises his deathbed to an exceptional degree, however, so that death completely dominates the surrounding space. In art of an earlier period, this would probably have been attributed simply to a lack of technical competence; see, for instance, Figure 32.5, John Souch's *Sir Thomas Aston at the Deathbed of his Wife*. Delacroix did in fact secure the services of a specialist in perspective to map out the lines of the architecture in the painting: he admitted to difficulties with the rules of perspective. Given the contemporary dominance of the neoclassical aesthetic, however, it is likely that the issues driving his approach went beyond matters of competence. In his painting the conventional, neoclassical horizontal format is subverted by the strong sense of diagonal movement. This subversion of compositional order is reminiscent of Goya's *St Francis Borja attending a Dying Impenitent* (Figure 32.6), in which the corpse, surrounded by blood and demons, appears to slide diagonally from a horizontal bed towards a dark foreground chasm, thus disrupting the underlying geometric framework. Delacroix had been introduced to Goya's work through his acquaintance in Paris with the Guillemardet family, whose father had served as ambassador in Spain. Earlier than most of his contemporaries, Delacroix became familiar with engravings of Goya's works, including the *Caprichos*, some of which you viewed in Video 2, band 1. It is unlikely that he knew the *St Francis Borja*, which had been a specific commission for Valencia Cathedral. It is highly probable, however, that Goya's work and style influenced Delacroix's works of the 1820s. Like Goya, Delacroix presents death in a way that challenges the static compositions of Neoclassicism.

The female nudes in *The Death of Sardanapalus* are of the curvaceous, fleshy, wild-haired type favoured by Rubens, slightly streamlined for a contemporary audience. We can see in the work the influence of

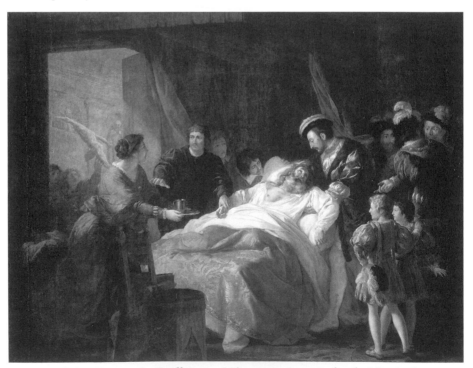

Figure 32.3   François Guillaume Ménageot, Leonardo de Vinci, dying in the Arms of Francis the First, *Amboise Château, Amboise. Photo: © RMN.*

Figure 32.4 Rembrandt van Rijn, The Death of the Virgin, *1639, pen and ink on paper, 40.9 x 31.5 cm, Leeds Museums and Galleries (City Art Gallery). Photo: Bridgeman Art Library.*

Rubens's *Landing of Maria de' Medici at Marseilles* (1621–5) (Plate 32.6 in the Illustrations Book). The standing nude in the foreground of Delacroix's painting was painted from life, but was influenced by a nereid (sea-nymph) in Rubens's *Landing* as well as by one of the nudes in his *Rape of the Daughters of Leucippus* (Plate 32.7) The shoulder and upper arm of the man stabbing Delacroix's nude were possibly influenced by the Triton (sea-god) in the left foreground of the *Landing*. These fleshy women are of a very different kind from the sleek, elongated nudes of Ingres (see his *Grande Odalisque*, Plate 32.8). The neoclassical was both linear and idealist in its approach. Ingres's nudes are not only clearly contoured, but also the result of a Platonic conception of beauty (see Block 4, Unit 16) which operated via a careful selection of elements from nature and the elimination of defects. It was not until the 1830s, however, that critics and commentators confronted the stylistic gulf that separated Delacroix from Ingres (see Carrington Shelton, 2000, p.728).

Rubens represents a very different interpretation of 'the classical' from that favoured by the neoclassicists. His history paintings often use the luminous diagonals (shafts of light falling diagonally across the canvas), turbulent movement, luscious colour and sparkling objects that exerted such a profound influence on Delacroix, as on many other Romantic

Figure 32.5   John Souch, Sir Thomas Aston at the Deathbed of his Wife, *1635, oil on canvas, 215.1 x 203.2 cm, City Art Gallery, Manchester. © Manchester Art Gallery.*

Figure 32.6   Francisco de Goya, St Francis Borja attending a Dying Impenitent, *1788, oil on canvas, 300 x 350 cm, Valencia Cathedral, Spain. Photo: Bridgeman Art Library.*

artists (see Block 4, Unit 17). It is interesting to speculate on the reasons for Delacroix's preferences. They were probably, in part, temperamental: following the example of Rubens would have allowed him to work in a more painterly manner, with freer brushstrokes and with less fear of the laws of geometry and of the precision of a clear contour that had been so important in the works of Poussin and other sources for Neoclassicism. Also, in this case the style suits the subject: what better way to represent a collapsing regime than by means of a compositional technique that encapsulates collapse? The 'orgy' of colour is also appropriate to the subject, but was equally controversial.

EXERCISE   Compare the effects of colour and light in *Sardanapalus* with those in David's *Andromache mourning Hector* (Plate 32.3 in the Illustrations Book). What similarities and differences can you see? (You may find it helpful to look also at Plates 32.9–32.12, preparatory works for Delacroix's painting.)

DISCUSSION   Both paintings contain highly coloured areas, but these are more dominant in Delacroix's work than in David's. The boy in David's painting wears a bright red cloak, but this is a relatively modest colour note in a generally moderately coloured work. In Delacroix's painting there are darker, more restrained areas – for example, in the top right-hand corner – but (and this is a lot easier to see in the original) much of the canvas is dominated by red and gold so that the general effect is opulent. David's quieter colour harmonies do not distract from the linear and intellectual appeal of the image. Delacroix uses colour in a more assertive way, not only to unify his painting but also to create an overall sensuousness.

In David's painting the grieving Andromache is very dramatically highlighted by a spotlight effect, which helps to focus our attention. In *Sardanapalus* several figures are highlighted so that there is no obvious focal point. These patches of light, like many of the figures in the painting, which result from individual studies (see Plates 32.9–32.12), remain distinct and separate from one another. (This is incidentally a departure from the traditional academic process of using broad areas of light and shadow to unify a painting and direct the viewer's eye towards a primary figure.) In David's canvas Andromache provides a centre of emotional and visual interest, but the bright light falling on her unites with and flows into the gentler light illuminating Hector. In Delacroix's painting it is areas of colour, rather than the suggestion of light falling on objects, that glue together the various areas of the composition.

A sensuous use of colour subverted the neoclassical aesthetic, in which moral and intellectual messages – or, at the very least, a concept of 'noble form' – were intended to dominate. In the case of Delacroix, this attention to the effects of colour is heightened by a concern with the textural qualities of paint. In order to produce a matt but bright surface, he applied thin layers of oil glaze to an initial **lay-in** of **distemper** (see ten-Doesschate Chu, 2001, p.102). It is thought that he was aiming to produce an effect similar to that of pastels and watercolours – many of his preliminary studies for the painting are in pastels. Indeed, Delacroix learned from various other artists. For example, he established a firm friendship with Richard Parkes Bonington, the English watercolourist. He later recalled how he and Bonington had met in around 1816, when Bonington was working on studies in the gallery of the Louvre. The two artists met again when Delacroix visited England in 1825 and later shared a studio in Paris. Delacroix admired and tried to emulate the lightness of touch and sparkle of Bonington's technique (see Plate 32.13 in the Illustrations Book).

Whereas neoclassical work aimed to preserve a smoothed-down paint surface produced by the use of delicate, fine brushstrokes, Delacroix applied to the finished canvas of *Sardanapalus* a technique called flossing. Possibly borrowed from Constable, whose *Haywain* Delacroix had seen in the Salon of 1824, this process involves the application of short delicate strokes of colour on top of the 'finished' paint surface and enhances the impression of sparkling light. This clearly demonstrates Delacroix's adventurous approach to technique. He also borrowed from Constable, in this and earlier works, the method of applying thin colour cross-hatchings to distemper in order to achieve his shadows. Traditionally, shadows had been painted as thin, dark glazes, with no colour interest at all: they had had a muddy, dirty effect, as the local (actual) colour of an object had been mixed with black. Constable and Delacroix revolutionized the painting of shadow by representing it as composed of strands of colour. This was a far cry from conventional academic chiaroscuro.[5]

Rubens versus Poussin, colour versus line – these were the polarities around which much debate in France had been structured since the late seventeenth century, when the Royal Academy of Painting had been founded. The defence of line or contour had been linked with idealization and the idea of absolute, perfect beauty derived from drawing skills based on observation of antique statuary. Colour had been associated with the emotive and the sensual and given less status: it satisfied the eye rather than the mind. This polarity was, of course, artificial. Most artists were concerned with both colour *and* line. It was therefore often a matter of perceived priorities. An article in the review *L'Artiste* of 1832 anticipated the Delacroix–Ingres polarity that would become well established from 1834 onwards:

---

[5] As you may remember from Block 4, chiaroscuro is the use of light and shade to model form (that is, to suggest the three-dimensional presence of objects and figures) or to create tonal effects, from the subtle to the dramatic.

It's the battle between antique and modern genius. M. Ingres belongs in many respects to the heroic age of the Greeks; he is perhaps more of a sculptor than a painter; he occupies himself exclusively with line and form, purposefully neglecting animation and colour ... M. Delacroix, in contrast, wilfully sacrifices the rigours of drawing to the demands of the drama he depicts; his manner, less chaste and reserved, more ardent and animated, emphasizes the brilliance of colour over the purity of line.

(Quoted in Carrington Shelton, 2000, pp.731–2)

The 'ardent and animated' aspects of Delacroix's work made commentators describe his large canvases of the 1820s as 'Romantic'. By the end of the decade, he was regarded by many younger artists as the leader of a new, modern school of painting that in a spirit of revolutionary fervour had thrown off the shackles of a worn-out classicism. And yet, when a stranger who had seen *Sardanapalus* referred to Delacroix as the 'Victor Hugo of painting', the artist responded, 'You are mistaken, Sir, I am a pure classicist' (quoted in Wilson-Smith, 1992, p.78). To put this in context: the 1827 *Preface to Cromwell* by the writer and critic Victor Hugo, an acknowledged leader of the Romantics, is a manifesto accompanying a drama he had written. It is a call to arms to fellow Romantics to cast aside the old ways and embrace a Romantic credo. The main thrust of the *Preface* is blatantly anti-classical: Hugo demands that writers should no longer work under the tyranny of classical rules or genres. Arguing that there must be a new spirit of liberty in art, he declares, 'There are no rules; there are no models! Or rather there are no rules except the general rules of nature' (Hugo, 1949, p.41). While he acknowledges that writers must proceed in a way compatible with their chosen subject, Hugo also denounces the servile imitation of any source. Delacroix was determined, in spite of all the criticism, to hold on to a good opinion of his controversial painting, but resented the suggested identification with this cutting-edge côterie. In the following section we'll look at some of the reasons behind this crisis of artistic identity. In the meantime, the main point to take away from this section is that Delacroix's painting of *Sardanapalus* was felt to be too extreme in its departure from the compositional and colour effects of neoclassical art.

Delacroix – classic or Romantic?

In this section I shall map out some of the aspects of Delacroix's early career that help to explain his approach in *Sardanapalus*.

Delacroix consistently asserted his allegiance to classicism, in the broadest sense of an interest in the history and culture of ancient Greece and Rome. It had played a significant part in his early education. As a boy he attended the Lycée Impérial in Paris, which was known, before and after the empire period, as the Collège Louis-le-Grand. There he was schooled in the classics, philosophy, history and literature, studying Latin and Greek authors, as well as French seventeenth-century classic literary works such as those of Racine and Corneille. From 1815 he studied in the studio of the neoclassicist Pierre-Narcisse Guérin, where he was immersed in subjects from antiquity (see Plate 32.14 in the Illustrations Book, Guérin's *The Return of Marcus Sextus*). Like his contemporaries, Delacroix regarded classicism as a matter not only of subject matter and content (the inclusion in a painting of sections of ancient Roman architecture, antique drapes and costumes, historical and mythological tales from antiquity) but also, as we have seen, of style. In Guérin's studio Delacroix learned the rudiments of a neoclassical style of painting. Guérin eventually became the director of the French Academy (of painting) in Rome, an appointment that demonstrated his approval by the establishment. From 1816 to 1822 Delacroix also attended classes at the École des Beaux-Arts, where he received further instruction in an academic, classical style of painting, making studies from plaster casts of antique sculpture. And throughout his life Delacroix visited and copied paintings in the Louvre by artists such as Rubens, Raphael, Correggio, Titian, Veronese and Rembrandt. These were all masters from whom student painters were expected to learn, even though they did not represent a cohesive classical tradition.

It was at the École des Beaux-Arts that Delacroix met Théodore Géricault, whose Romantic canvases, such as *The Raft of the Medusa* (Plate 32.15 in the Illustrations Book), made an impact on him. Delacroix posed as one of the foreground figures in this work, which was somewhat controversial due to its heroic and realistic treatment of a contemporary news story of French naval troops and settlers, shipwrecked on their way to Senegal and signalling to another vessel for help. The painting's departure from grand, literary and classical themes was regarded as a disturbing challenge to tradition, given its adoption of the scale and importance of history painting. The graphic, realistic portrayal of human suffering was an implicit challenge to classical idealization. In order to draw the bodies of the figures, the artist had made studies from actual corpses and severed limbs. Nevertheless, Géricault's essential inspiration remained the academic, classical nude (he had seen and admired work by Michelangelo). What he achieved was a radical reworking of classical norms. He massed together writhing figures into a composition, marked by dramatic diagonal lines, that threatens to topple the 'stable' classical pyramidal figure groups (one surmounted by a signalling figure, the other by a mast) it contains. The final result, a muscular and energetic reinterpretation of a classical style, provided an example that was to be well taken by Delacroix.

Géricault's challenge to prevailing notions of the 'classical' or 'classic' was among many that influenced the early career of Delacroix. You have already seen in Block 2, Unit 9 how, during the Napoleonic empire, Antoine-Jean Gros introduced a more flamboyant, colourist style that, in its treatment of scale and pictorial space, departed from neoclassical norms. Gros was later to regret what he saw as some of the misdirected energy of his youth, but Delacroix greatly admired him. He was able to view Gros's large Napoleonic canvases after the older artist had praised a painting discussed in more detail below, Delacroix's 1822 Salon entry, *The Barque of Dante* (Plate 32.16 in the Illustrations Book):

> I idolized Gros's talent, which still is for me at the time of this writing [that is, at the end of Delacroix's life], and after everything that I have seen, one of the most remarkable in the history of painting. Pure chance led me to meeting Gros, who, learning that I was the painter of the picture in question, complimented me with such unbelievable warmth that for the rest of my life I have been immune to all flattery. He ended by telling me, after bringing out all its merits, that it was a *polished Rubens*. For him, who adored Rubens and who had been brought up in the severe school of David, it was the highest of praise. He asked me if he could do anything for me. I asked him forthwith to let me see his famous paintings of the Empire, which at that time were in the obscurity of his workshop, since they could not be openly exhibited because of the times [restoration France] and because of their subjects. He left me there for four hours, alone or with him, in the middle of his sketches, his preliminary works.
>
> (Quoted in Jobert, 1998, pp.68–9)

Another influence on Delacroix, as we have seen, was Rubens, who represented a particular strain of classicism often referred to as Baroque. This term was first applied to painting by nineteenth-century art historians. It carries overtones of the capricious and the florid, and is used of a style of painting dating roughly from the late Renaissance to the end of the seventeenth century. Rubens had studied and copied ancient Roman statues, friezes and tombs. He made drawings that are as austere in their linear classicism as those of any artist, and he painted the religious and mythological subjects expected of classical art. However, he moved on to paint figures that are more fleshy and realistic than statuesque, and came to prefer dramatic to static compositions. Here is one recent attempt, by newspaper critic Brian Sewell, to sum up the Baroque style. Sewell responds impatiently to what he perceives to be inadequate definitions:

> Baroque composition is, in essence, a construction based on logic and perspective, but so swept away by serpentine lines and dramatic diagonals (and so co-ordinated by them), so daring in strenuous movements towards and away from the spectator that the frame and picture plane seem scarcely able to contain them; in extreme Baroque pictures elements swirl and flow as though subject to some cosmic force, contrasts of light and shadow are employed to add both drama and realism, and every constituent is seen to be a support for the core subject, no matter how remote from it.
>
> (Sewell, 2001)

This Baroque energy is evident in Rubens, but it also features, less explicitly, in the work of artists not normally characterized as Baroque. For example, in the Bacchanalian revels painted by Nicolas Poussin in *A Bacchanalian Revel before a Term*[6] and in his *Rape of the Sabines* (see Plates 32.17 and 32.18 in the Illustrations Book), diagonal movement, drama and vivid colour are imposed on more conventional classical settings in order to produce an effect very different from that of his *Testament of Eudamidas* (see Figure 32.1). Some of Poussin's clients required this colourist, dramatic style: his 'pure' classicism was susceptible to Baroque adaptation, although you may have noticed the clearly controlled linearity that remains in his *Bacchanalian Revel*. In these works by Poussin, the movement and the colour are controlled with a balanced and harmonious composition. As, from the seventeenth century onwards, French aesthetic preferences polarized around Poussin and Rubens (perceived champions, respectively, of line and colour), the argument was largely one of *degree*: the proportion of swirling movement and colour to balance, order, contour and harmony. The late nineteenth-century philosopher Nietzsche characterized Greek tragedy, and indeed all art, as a tension between the Dionysiac (Bacchanalian forces of whirling revelry, after Dionysus, the Greek god of wine) and the Apolline (the forces of poetic harmony, order and reason, after Apollo, the Greek god of beauty, civilization and the arts). This tension is evident in Delacroix's painting, as the Apolline neoclassical comes under attack from the Romantic Dionysiac: the lack of obvious focal point or compositional unity seems to drive his work even beyond the Baroque. For many contemporaries, *Sardanapalus* had got the balance wrong, and much of the remainder of Delacroix's career aimed to address this. He did not, however, follow the neoclassicists Gérard, Guérin and Ingres. While aiming for more ordered compositions, he continued to see Michelangelo and Rubens as the sources of a classicism more muscular, dynamic and vital than that championed by the Academy and David's followers. He sought a more expressive classicism, better adapted to the prevailing culture of the Romantic:

> Delacroix's pictorial practice was shaped by conflict. Aiming at both simplicity of effect and a richness of colour and texture, striving for the calm of Veronese and the turbulence of Rubens, Delacroix was forever torn between his classic sense of order and his innate Romantic impulse. To resolve that conflict was the driving force of his art.
>
> (ten-Doesschate Chu, 2001, p.107)

The urge to depart from tradition, without abandoning classicism, is apparent in Delacroix's earliest Salon exhibits. Displayed there in 1822, some years before the *Sardanapalus*, *The Barque of Dante* (see Plate 32.16 in the Illustrations Book) depicts an episode from the *Inferno*, a

---

[6] A 'term' in this context is a bust placed on a tapered pillar.

poem written by the medieval Italian poet Dante. The poet imagines being rowed, in the company of the Roman poet Virgil, across the lake surrounding the infernal city of Dis, which is in flames in the background. Sinners are clinging to and trying to climb into the boat. The work, not commissioned and on a subject of Delacroix's own choice, was bought by the government for its museum of modern art, the Musée du Luxembourg. Although it does not conform to the practices of Neoclassicism, its use of tonal effects and nudes is very similar to that of Michelangelo, an alternative classical source. It lies recognizably within the tradition of grand history painting, and the composition (with symmetrical, central figures surrounded by a balanced arrangement of other figures) is classical. As we saw earlier, Gros regarded it as a 'polished Rubens'. Its use of colour is novel but fairly restrained. There is a mass of grey enlivened by skilfully placed patches of green, red and blue. Influenced by Rubens's *Landing of Maria de' Medici at Marseilles* (Plate 32.6), the droplets of water on the nudes' bodies show all the colours of the spectrum. (The work was retouched in 1859, however, so we must take care in our assumptions about what was in the 'original'.) Rubens had certainly established a tradition of dramatic seascapes (see Plate 32.19, *The Miracle of St Walburga*). Charles Delécluze found Delacroix's painting as a whole a 'real mess' (quoted in Jobert, 1998, p.69), but admired the drawing and colour of the main figures. In a review of the 1822 Salon, however, Adolphe Thiers saw the work as evidence of Delacroix's genius: 'I find this power wild, ardent but natural, which effortlessly yields to its own force ... I do not think I am wrong: M. Delacroix has the gift of genius' (quoted in Jobert, 1998, p.69). With his first Salon, Delacroix thus gained a reputation as an innovator who worked within, rather than overthrowing, tradition. The choice of subject was novel for a history painter and showed a departure from the usual repertoire of topics from classical antiquity and national history.

If the *Barque* had marked Delacroix out as an innovator, his next important Salon exhibit, *Massacres of Chios* (1824) (see Plate 9.2 in the Illustrations Book), was much bolder in its challenge to the establishment. The painting, which you have already met in Block 2, Unit 9, is a fictionalized account of the aftermath of the Turks' massacre of 20,000 Greeks on the island of Chios, which occurred in 1822 during the Greek Wars of Independence. The massacre was a reprisal for Turkish losses caused by a Greek uprising against Turkish occupation. Again the painting was not commissioned and depicts a subject of Delacroix's own choosing. It was exhibited at the 1824 Salon, where it won a medal. Although the painting does not conform to the neoclassical norm, there are aspects of its composition which are classical. The figures, for example, are grouped into triangles or pyramids, and there is an overall sense of balance – disrupted slightly on the right-hand side by the Turk rearing up on his horse, literally dominating the Greek victims. Unconventionally, however, in place of the centralized hero or object of interest of a classical composition, there is a gaping hole that allows a view on to distant hills. This lack of a hero, of a visual centre and of a unity of interest (the figures seem singularly uninterested in one another) subverted the normal conventions of history painting. Many critics found the subject too ugly, the figures too cold, passive and defeated, and the technique too rough, disjointed and jarring.

For one critic loyal to the Davidian school, Pierre-Athanase Chauvin, this was all too much. He regarded Delacroix's work as the ultimate Romantic insult to classical beauty:

> It is not to arrest the development of our young artists that I am so quick to indicate the steps by which a distinguished painter, the teacher of their teachers [David], led the historical genre to the apogee of its glory; it is rather to establish a necessary point of comparison, which ought to humiliate no one; it is, in short, to avoid the words 'classic' and 'romantic', or, if you will, to explain them clearly and precisely. The classic is drawn from *la belle nature*; it touches us, it moves us, it satisfies heart and mind together. The more one studies, the more one discovers its beauties; one leaves it with regret, and returns to it with pleasure. The romantic, on the contrary, has something forced, unnatural, which at first glance shocks the eye and upon examination repels it. The artist, in delirium, uselessly combines atrocious scenes, sheds blood, tears out innards, paints despair and agony. Uselessly again, he obtains partial effects in the midst of a thousand extravagances, and makes people who know nothing about it shout, 'Miracle!' Posterity will never accept such works, and contemporaries of good faith will grow weary of them; they are weary already. Conclusion: I call *Leonidas* [a painting by David] ... classic, and the *Massacres of Chios* romantic.

(Quoted in Jobert, 1998, pp.75–6)

Chauvin viewed both Delacroix's subject and his technique as barbaric: the painting dealt with no eternal truths and delivered no inspiring lesson. Other complaints were voiced about the rough brushwork that called attention to itself in such a non-academic manner. The 'cadaverous tint' of the bodies also drew criticism. Gros, whose own compositional experiments had inspired Delacroix, allegedly called the picture the 'massacre of painting' (quoted in Johnson, 1981, p.87), while Stendhal, aware of the influence of Gros and (probably) disappointed by the lack of overt heroism in the work, said the 'massacre' was more like a 'plague' (quoted in Wright, 2001, p.32) – in Delacroix's painting, the red-rimmed eyes of the old woman are derived from Gros's *Bonaparte Visiting the Plague-Stricken of Jaffa* (see Plate 9.15 in the Illustrations Book). However, the use of colour in Delacroix's work is again adventurous and reflects the influence of Rubens. There are coloured shadows (for example in the shadow cast by the old woman's wide sleeve) and a striking balancing of complementary reds and greens, blues and yellows. This use of complementaries to generate colour interest and contrast was taken to new lengths by Delacroix. The general colour key of the landscape, however, is light and fresh, influenced by Constable and Bonington. Before the Salon opened, and having just seen some paintings by Constable destined for the same exhibition, Delacroix retouched his painting using fine brushstrokes, additional glazes, highlights and varnish to make the surface sparkle. Some commentators found the colours too bright and clashing. Although certain artists, such as Gérard and Girodet, did admire the painting, it created the kind of furore that was by now associated by conservative critics with attention-seeking Romantics. The choice of a contemporary, topical subject raised similar suspicions: in the academic classical tradition, subjects were usually drawn from a literary, mythological or historical past that could be viewed from a safe distance. The fact, however, that the government awarded Delacroix a medal and subsequently bought the painting shows that it was capable of occasional liberal and innovative insight. The picture had caused a stir and the artist was seen as a rising star, irrespective of the carping criticism he attracted. Government medals provided a means of acknowledging, rather than approving, an artist's achievement.

Much of the ground for the reception of *Sardanapalus* had now been prepared. The classic–Romantic divide, with David's followers on one side and Gros and Géricault on the other, was already well established by the time Delacroix produced his painting of mass suicide. Contemporary viewers would have detected Romantic allegiances in, for example, the horse and black slave, probably influenced by Gros. And yet Delacroix never came to terms with the perception of himself as the enemy of classicism. It bothered him that he should be regarded as someone out of control, swept along by the energies and eddies of an uncontrollable genius. He was stung by reactions to what he perceived as a generally successful work:

> I am sick of this whole Salon. They'll end by making me believe that I've had a real fiasco. And yet I'm not entirely convinced. Some say it's a total failure, that *The Death of Sardanapalus* means the death of the Romantics, since that's what they call us; others bluntly declare that I'm *inganno* [in error], but that they'd rather be wrong with me than be right like a thousand others who have good sense on their side, if you like, but who deserve damnation in the name of the soul and of the imagination. My own opinion is that they're all idiots, that this picture has both qualities and faults, and that if there are some things in it that I could wish better done, there are plenty of others that I hold myself fortunate to have done and that they might well wish to have equalled ... It's all quite pitiful and would not deserve a moment's attention except in so far as it directly jeopardizes my wholly material interests, in other words, *cash*.

> (Letter to Charles Soulier, Paris, 11 March 1828, in Stewart, 1971, pp.145–6)

This final remark by Delacroix was prompted, perhaps, by the fact that he saw the state as the only realistic purchaser of a painting of this grandeur. Indeed, this was the situation faced by most history painters of the day working outside the remit of Church or private commissions. The artist's journal shows him to be a shrewd book-keeper, market researcher and businessman. Far from considering himself the witless victim of artistic delirium, Delacroix was, by the mid-1820s, an accomplished socialite – a regular attender at Parisian salons, acquiring expertise in the kind of self-publicity that would flourish later in his career. He assumed the role and appearance of an English dandy, undemonstrative and impassive (see Figure 32.7). Furthermore, his method of producing paintings was painstaking and founded on fine judgement: he usually made preparatory sketches, both compositional and of individual figures, based on the observation of models. In other words, his work does include a measure of the refined study of nature, control and intelligence expected of the classical artist. You may remember from Block 1, Unit 2 that Mozart's art was defined by later commentators as 'Classical' in order to distinguish it from the preceding Baroque style of music. We can see from this how each art form develops its own way of allocating labels to styles. Delacroix greatly admired Mozart's music, preferring it to Beethoven's, whose 'wild originality' was legendary. Beethoven's music was, he felt, 'obscure and ... lacking in unity' – the reason being that Beethoven 'turns his back on eternal principles: Mozart never' (quoted in Vaughan, 1978, p.246). The eternal and the unifying: these were the hallmarks of classical order and composition. While Delacroix did admire, in the work of musicians, artists and writers such as Beethoven, Rubens and Shakespeare, qualities of sketchiness and the unfinished, he nevertheless felt that the consummate, classical art of Racine and Mozart represented a form of eternal beauty (Hannoosh, 1995, pp.71–4).

EXERCISE   In order to sum up your work on this section, jot down some notes on how Delacroix's early career might be seen as moving away from a respect for the classical tradition and for the reason and order demanded of classical composition.

DISCUSSION   Delacroix's early education and training were dominated by the classical tradition. When he began to exhibit works at the Salon, he retained some aspects of classical composition (order, symmetry, the use of academic nudes). However, he worked within a tradition of Baroque classicism, which made him stand out from the neoclassicists of his age, and as the Baroque aspects of his work intensified, he became vulnerable to the charge of abandoning what was seen as a correct or pure form of the classical for Romanticism.

Figure 32.7   Eugène Delacroix, Self-Portrait, c.*1837, oil on canvas, 65 x 54.5 cm, Louvre, Paris. Photo:* © *RMN/J.G. Berizzi.*

Clearly, there came a point at which Baroque classicism redefined itself, in the eyes of contemporaries, as Romanticism. This was because, as a style, it became associated with a host of ideas about artistic creativity and about the role of art in the broader culture. Like Goethe's *Faust* (see Block 6, Units 26–27), Delacroix's painting seems to transcend the classic–Romantic divide. In the next section we shall look at the reasons why Delacroix's contemporaries placed him in the Romantic camp.

3   The Romantic artist and the creative process

In a journal entry of October 1822 Delacroix expressed the view that artists, unlike writers, don't have to say everything explicitly:

> The writer says nearly everything to be understood. In painting a mysterious bond is established between the souls of the sitters[7] and those of the spectator. He sees the faces, external nature; but he thinks inwardly the true thought that is common to all people, to which some give body in writing, yet altering its fragile essence. Thus grosser spirits are more moved by writers than by musicians and painters.
>
> (Pach, 1938, p.41)

This notion of the artist mediating between the souls of his models and those of his spectators lay at the heart of the Romantic aesthetic. Also central to Romanticism, as you have seen earlier (in Block 6, Units 24–25), was the idea that the artist dealt essentially with the inexplicit, with the suggested rather than with the clearly expressed. To the Romantics, sculpture was inferior to painting because of its material status: solid and three-dimensional, it was too close to real life and too explicit in its mode of representing our experience of the world. Music, on the other hand, enjoyed a special status since it excelled in inexplicit evocation. For the same reason, the sketch, as a means of artistic expression, came to enjoy a higher status: it was even less specific than a finished painting in its powers of evocation and in its ability to generate meaning. For Delacroix and the Romantics, this lack of specificity facilitated a deeper, primal process of communication. To his contemporaries, therefore, well acquainted with such views, the sketchiness or (apparently) rough brushwork of Delacroix's works signified a Romantic mindset. We have already seen, in Block 4, Unit 17, how both Turner and Constable used the sweeping brushstroke innovatively in the context of the dominant aesthetic of the classical picturesque and how this technique was seen as a means of gaining access to the artist's individual identity. Romantic artists such as Turner, Constable and Delacroix were, in this respect, exploring and engaging with a phenomenon that had been rationally identified and analysed, if not practised, by Enlightenment theorists.

Even William Gilpin, whose own artistic practice was so formula-bound, recognized the importance of leaving something to the imagination. In his *Observations ... on ... the Mountains, and Lakes of Cumberland, and Westmoreland,* he remarks:

> We may be pleased with the description, and the picture: but the soul can *feel* neither, unless the force of our own imagination aid the poet's, or the painter's art; exalt the idea; and *picture things unseen.*
>
> (Gilpin, 1973, vol.II, p.11)

---

[7] The French word used is *personnages* (see Joubin, 1996, p.29), which might alternatively be rendered as 'figures'.

Gilpin considered that sketches, unlike finished works, offer the imagination the opportunity to 'create something more itself' (1973, vol.II, p.16). Although he was suspicious of artists who let their imaginations roam too far from the 'simple standard of nature, in it's [*sic*] most beautiful forms', he nevertheless glimpsed in passing the potential of a less constrained approach to creativity. Similarly, the Enlightenment art critic, Denis Diderot, had distinguished between clay models and finished sculptures, the former being much closer to the initial moment of feeling and inspiration:

> The artist puts his fire into the clay, then when he goes at the stone boredom and indifference set in, the boredom and indifference adhere to the chisel and penetrate the marble, unless the sculptor is possessed of an inextinguishable zeal like that the old poet [Homer] attributed to his gods.

(Quoted in Goodman, 1995, p.170)

Once again, then, we see how the Romantics put into practice some of the possibilities perceived intellectually in the Enlightenment: the development from one to the other was an organic process. For instance, Delacroix's *The Murder of the Bishop of Liège* (1829) (see Plate 32.20 in the Illustrations Book) depicts an episode from a novel by Sir Walter Scott, *Quentin Durward* (1823). It shows the Bishop of Liège about to have his throat cut by rebels in his château, which has recently been captured by William de la Marck, 'the Boar of Ardennes', who now stands in front of the bishop and gives the order for him to be murdered on the spot. The painting is more 'finished' than the sketch which preceded it (see Plate 32.21), yet some critics found that it retained too much of the looseness of a sketch in, for example, the faces of the foreground figures. Like Turner and Constable, Delacroix retains in his paintings something of the original 'fire' of the sketch.

Although in public Delacroix assumed the demeanour of the accomplished socialite (he dined regularly with Hugo, Alfred de Musset and other writers, and was friendly with Chopin and George Sand, among others), his letters and journal entries speak of a keen sensitivity that, he believed, infused his art and set him apart from 'the common herd':

> As soon as a man is intelligent, his first duty is to be honest and strong. It is no use to try to forget, there is something virtuous in him that demands to be obeyed and satisfied. What do you think has been the life of men who have raised themselves above the common herd? Constant strife. Struggle against the idleness that is common to them and to the average man, when it is a question of writing, if he is a writer: because his genius clamors to be manifested; and it is not merely through some vain lust to be famed that he obeys it – it is through conscience. Let those who work lukewarmly be silent: what do they know of work dictated

by inspiration? This fear, this dread of awakening the slumbering lion, whose roarings stir your very being. To sum up: be strong, simple, and true; there is your problem for all times, and it is always useful.

(Pach, 1938, p.94)

Delacroix was dedicated to hard work and the conquering of natural idleness. The extract above from his journal shows how a large part of that work involved an authentic expression of the 'slumbering lion' of inspiration. This involved suffering. The notion of the solitary, suffering artist was familiar to the Romantic côterie of Delacroix's day. Delacroix himself captured the type in a painting entitled *Torquato Tasso in the Hospital of Saint Anna, Ferrara* (1824). In this painting Tasso, the sixteenth-century Italian poet and author of *Jerusalem Liberated*, an epic about the crusades, is confined to the madhouse. Tasso's status as persecuted, misunderstood artist is implicit in the story told in a play by Goethe translated into French in 1823. The poet was locked up because of his love for the sister of the Duke of Ferrara. The type of the solitary genius is also expressed in Delacroix's later *Michelangelo in his Studio* (1849–50) and in his portrait of Paganini (1831) (see Plates 32.22 and 32.23 in the Illustrations Book), as well as in the work of one of the artist's favourite writers, Byron:

> To fly from, need not be to hate, mankind.
> All are not fit with them to stir and toil,
> Nor is it discontent to keep the mind
> Deep in its fountain, lest it overboil
> In the hot throng.

(*Childe Harold's Pilgrimage*, Canto III, line lxix)

Expressing one's identity and inspiration was not simply, however, a matter of spontaneity, of (for example) dashes of paint transferring to the canvas an inner essence or soul. In a Romantic work, and contrary to the pronouncements of many critics, nothing could be so transparent, not even the identity of the artist – you may recall from Block 6, Units 29–30 that quintessential quality of the Byronic, the 'secret language' in which only special souls may share.

EXERCISE   Read the following extract (dating from May 1824) from Delacroix's journal. From 1822, following Rousseau's tradition of self-confession, Delacroix kept a diary in which he expressed his views on himself and on his art. It was not published until 1893–5. What view does Delacroix express here about revealing one's inner being in art?

> What torments my soul is its loneliness. The more it expands among friends and the daily habits or pleasures, the more, it seems to me, it flees me and retires into its fortress. The poet

who lives in solitude, but who produces much, is the one who enjoys those treasures we bear in our bosom, but which forsake us when we give ourselves to others. When one yields oneself completely to one's soul, it opens itself completely to one, and then it is that the capricious thing allows one of the greatest of good fortunes ... that of sympathizing with others, of studying itself, of painting itself constantly in its works, something that Byron and Rousseau have perhaps not noticed. I am not talking about mediocre people: for what is this rage, not only to write, but to be published? Outside of the happiness of being praised, there is that of addressing all souls that can understand yours, and so it comes to pass that all souls meet in your painting.

(Pach, 1938, p.89)

DISCUSSION   An artist who 'yields' to his soul may express it in his art and hence communicate with other 'souls that can understand yours'. This is, however, best achieved (paradoxically) from a position of solitude. (You may recall from Block 6, Units 24–25 Wackenroder's similar insistence on the separation of aesthetic experience from everyday life.) Effective expression of one's inner being is dependent on the adequate understanding of others.

In another journal entry of 1824, Delacroix speaks of the fact that the soul is inevitably trapped within the physical body:

It seems to me that the body may be the organization that tones down the soul, which is more universal, yet passes through the brain as through a rolling mill which hammers it and stamps it with the stamp of our insipid physical nature, and what weight is more insufferable than that of this living cadaver which we inhabit? Instead of dashing towards the objects of desire that it cannot grasp, nor even define, it spends the flashing instant of life submitting to the stupid situations into which this tyrant throws it. As a bad joke, doubtless, heaven has allowed us to view the sight of the world through this absurd window: its fieldglass, out of focus and lustreless, always turned in the same direction, spoils all the judgments of the other, whose native good faith is often corrupted and often horrible fruits are the result!

(Pach, 1938, p.93)

So far, then, we can see how Delacroix's Romantic view of the artist as an elite soul was mediated by the 'bad joke' of his sensuality and physical weaknesses – 'A link reluctant in a fleshly chain' (Byron, *Childe Harold's Pilgrimage*, Canto III, line lxxii). You might recall, in this context, the discussion in Units 24–25 on Romantic wit – on the impossibility of expressing through finite, material means the infinite and the immaterial. All of this might support the view that *Sardanapalus* is a sensuous riot entrapping (yet revealing to the initiated) the artist's soul. But there was another force that Delacroix found to be of essential importance to the artist: intelligence or reason. The Enlightenment had typically expressed, on the one hand, the soul and imagination and, on the other, reason and intelligence in terms of incompatible opposites. Not so Delacroix:

> What are the soul and the intelligence when separated? The pleasure of naming and classifying is the fatal thing about men of learning. They are always overreaching themselves and spoiling their game in the eyes of those easy-going, fair-minded people who believe that nature is an impenetrable veil. I know very well that in order to agree about things, we must name them; but henceforth they are specified.
>
> (Pach, 1938, pp.93–4)

The view that the world is essentially an 'impenetrable veil' rather than a composite of knowable, classifiable and understandable phenomena will be familiar to you from Units 24–25. It represents a key shift from Enlightenment to Romantic thinking. But note how, in this Romantic statement of belief in the world as an 'impenetrable veil' concealing a deeper reality and apparently defying rational understanding, Delacroix does not abandon the notion of intelligence or reason so dear to the Enlightenment. Rather, he incorporates it into the inseparable whole of his artistic identity. His intelligence fuses with his 'soul'. The Romantics broke some of the boundaries and fixed categories which the Enlightenment had been keen to establish. In this case, it is significant that Delacroix sees intelligence as part of his innermost being, trapped, with his 'soul', within a physical body. In his paintings, therefore, we must expect some concealment of the self, imperfectly expressed through the sensuous and the physical and mediated by the workings of the intellect. No wonder he was so dismayed when viewers saw *Sardanapalus* as nothing more than an orgy of sex and violence: they showed no willingness to penetrate the 'veil', as it were. A sceptic in matters of religion, Delacroix held views on art that nevertheless assumed the existence of something beneath and beyond the purely material. And yet we must not forget the possibility that Delacroix's journal may be, above all, a skilful work of self-presentation and self-justification.

Romantic themes and subjects in Delacroix's art

Many of Delacroix's contemporaries found the subject matter of his *Sardanapalus* excessive and unpalatable. This was the opinion of an anonymous reviewer in the *Moniteur Universel* on 29 January 1828, who expressed the view that 'the name [of Sardanapalus] has become synonymous with all that is most ridiculous and vile about debauchery and cowardice'. Furthermore, it was unlikely that 'an effeminate prince should magically become a tactician and a warrior capable of defending Nineveh' (quoted in Spector, 1974, p.80). Delacroix's subject disturbed because it was the precise antithesis of classical heroism. Sardanapalus appears to be the ultimate anti-hero, world-weary, defeated, egotistical. Stendhal, while admiring Delacroix's energy, was disturbed by the 'satanism' of the painting. Such interpretations were reinforced by, for example, the dark, hellish chasm at the bottom of the picture, which might be compared to the waters in the *Barque of Dante*. The painting shows an absolute ruler about to go up in flames with more than a lifetime's provision of sex and violence. Here is no military hero or ruler offering a moral example, but a death scene worthy of Don Giovanni or the Marquis de Sade's dying man – both of whom you encountered in Block 1 – and (implicitly) uncomprehending of the kind of rational assessment of suicide that David Hume would have recommended. The moral clarity and certitudes of Neoclassicism, born of the Enlightenment and perpetuated in revolutionary ideology, have given way to a futile, self-defeating hedonism.

For many of Delacroix's Romantic contemporaries, versed in Byronic despondency and melancholic ruminations on the futility and transitory nature of worldly pleasure, *Sardanapalus* expressed the condition of *ennui*[8] – a kind of inner emptiness, languor, stultification and world-weariness. When painting his later *Liberty Leading the People* (Plate 32.28 in the Illustrations Book), which is discussed further below, Delacroix admitted that the hard work he did on it banished his 'spleen',[9] another word used by the Romantics to suggest a lack of interest in life, or melancholy humour (see Johnson, 1981, p.130). Like Faust, the artist fought against inertia and the temptations of nihilism. He confessed, in a journal entry of May 1824, that he needed to abandon reason and stir up his mind in order to satisfy its 'black depth'. We might almost see *Sardanapalus* as reinforcing a Rousseauesque diatribe against luxury or acquisitiveness. While many Enlightenment thinkers (including Voltaire) had seen luxury as a sign of advanced civilization, Rousseau had regarded it as a symbol of moral and social corruption and had urged a return to more natural, primitive values. In Byron's play, Sardanapalus

---

[8] This term had been used in medieval French to signify profound sadness, disgust and personal anguish. From the seventeenth century onwards it was used to describe a vaguer, less powerful form of melancholy or listlessness. See *Le Robert*, 2000, vol.I, p.745.

[9] The word 'spleen' had been borrowed from English and was used by French writers from the eighteenth century onwards. It carried associations with the black humours or bile created by the bodily organ of the same name, attributed by the ancients with the power to create illness and melancholy.

refers to the prospect of being 'purified by death from some/Of the gross stains of too material being' (Gordon, 1970, p.491). We are reminded, also, of William Wilberforce's criticism of 'rapacity ... venality ... sensuality' (see Anthology I, p.286). Apparently, then, the painting subverts the materialistic impulses behind the Royal Pavilion at Brighton and other sumptuous palaces. Delacroix's particular Romantic sensibility is expressed as the denial of desire, or the searing realization of the ultimate inadequacy of the material and the sensuous.

Most of the subjects Delacroix painted in the 1820s broke free from the constraints of the morally uplifting themes of the classical tradition, which had focused on the heroic and sacred achievements of ancient Greece and Rome or the saints and martyrs of Christianity. In the historical romances of Sir Walter Scott, the Gothic, medieval and anecdotal took the place of the grand, universal ideas that underpinned much classical art. There was a thriving private market for such subjects, which challenged the dominance in the Academy of classical history and culture. You may recall from Block 6, Units 24–25 how legends, myths and tales were valued by the Romantics for their embodiment of valuable, imaginative truths. Delacroix was always proud of the daring approach he adopted in *Sardanapalus* – if saddened, ultimately, by the charge of defection from classicism uttered by those viewing it. He had written **Gothic novels** in his youth. His Gothic paintings, with their dark, looming architecture and horrifying events (as in *The Murder of the Bishop of Liège*), contrast with the order and decorum of David's Neoclassicism; they liberated the artist's imagination from an exhausted classical repertoire.

Indeed, a taste for the Gothic permeated French popular taste of the 1820s. Novellas and stage melodramas based on Gothic horror were in vogue. They frequently included stock figures of evil priests, monks and aristocrats: the Gothic was exploited as a means of social critique. In 1824 Delacroix made some caricature studies of priests and monks based on Goya's *Caprichos* series (see Plate 32.24 in the Illustrations Book, Goya's *They're Hot*, and Plates 32.25 and 32.26, sketches by Delacroix in similar vein). The plot of one of Delacroix's own Gothic novellas, *Alfred*, concerns a corrupt priest who persuades an evil nobleman to force his son to take monastic vows so that the son's inheritance may be easier to steal. Such plots were based on the darker side of Enlightenment literature, such as Diderot's *The Nun* (written in 1760), a tale of Gothic suffering and forced convent vows. Gothic literature and art revelled in the extreme and the spectacular, in evil, ugliness and all manner of Faustian pacts with the devil. *Sardanapalus*, with its satanic destruction and horror, might be viewed as the archetypal Gothic melodrama.

The grotesque was one aspect of this new aesthetic. The antithesis of the sublime and the beautiful, it was defined by Victor Hugo in his *Preface to Cromwell*:

> In the thinking of the moderns ... the grotesque plays a massive role. It is everywhere; on the one hand, it creates the deformed and the horrid; on the other, the comic and the farcical. It brings to religion thousands of original superstitious ideas and to poetry thousands of picturesque imaginings. It scatters and sows generously in air, water, earth and fire a myriad hybrid beings alive in popular medieval traditions; it is the grotesque that makes the terrifying circle of the [witches'] sabbath turn in the shadows, that gives Satan his horns, cloven hoofs and bat's wings. It is also the grotesque that ... hurls into Christians' hell those hideous figures later evoked by the grim genius of Dante and Milton ... If it turns from the ideal to the real, it performs there inexhaustible parodies of humanity. The creations of its fantasy are those Scaramouches, Crispins and Harlequins [well-known comic types of the Commedia dell'Arte], grimacing shadows of men, types totally unknown to grave antiquity and yet originating in classical Italy [ancient Roman drama]. It is, finally, the grotesque that, adding colour, by turns, to the imaginative drama of both the south and the north, makes Sganarelle prance about Don Juan [in a comedy by the French seventeenth-century dramatist Molière], Mephistopheles around Faust.

> (Hugo, 1949, p.27; trans. Walsh)

The 'picturesque imaginings' of the grotesque recall both the intense, hybrid interiors of Brighton Pavilion and the nightmare experiences recounted by Thomas De Quincey.

The Gothic and the grotesque replaced classical reason, order and regularity with the irrational, the irregular and the deformed. Delacroix was drawn to them as a means of breathing new life into artistic expression. He was attracted to English and German literature, particularly Shakespeare and Goethe – because, to the unified, clearly defined aesthetic categories of the classical, they opposed the fractured and hybrid genres less susceptible to categorization of any kind (see Block 6, Units 26–27 on *Faust*). Shakespeare mixed tragedy with comedy, and both he and Goethe, in some of their work at least, mixed beauty with the grotesque. The term 'grotesque' had originated as a means of describing the ornamentation discovered, during the Renaissance, in Roman grottoes. Originally it was coined in connection with ornate, fantasy figures, a mix of the real and the imaginary. To the enlightened, neoclassical architect Robert Adam, the grotesque was 'that beautiful light stile of ornament used by the ancient Romans, in the decoration of their palaces, baths and villas' (from *The Works in Architecture of Robert and James Adam, Esquires* (1778–1822), quoted in Eliot and Whitlock, 1992, vol.I, p.228) – in other words, a source of elegance. Then the term acquired connotations of the extravagant or ridiculous. Hugo meant by it anything strange, monstrous, ridiculous, comic, deformed, physically or morally ugly. To the Romantics of Delacroix's generation, the grotesque allowed them to cross traditional boundaries of the comic and the tragic in a way reminiscent of Mozart's *Don Giovanni*, a hybrid made up of *opera seria* and *opera buffa*. Its mix of the real and the theatrical, the extravagant and the serious also recalls the Gothic, neoclassical and exotic hybridity of the Royal Pavilion at Brighton, although this building (along with the equally heterodox poem *Lallah Rookh* by Thomas Moore) lacked the dark, satanic overtones often incorporated into the grotesque by French Romantics.

Delacroix also challenged tradition in paintings like *Greece on the Ruins of Missolonghi* (1826) and *Liberty Leading the People* (1830) (Plates 32.27 and 32.28 in the Illustrations Book), in which he mixes conventional, classical allegory with realism: the leading women in these paintings are both antique ideal and fleshy reality. (This rejection of traditional boundaries and categories was a hallmark of the Romantic mindset.) *Greece on the Ruins of Missolonghi* commemorates the death in 1824 of Byron at Missolonghi. Byron had travelled there in order to assist and finance Greek insurgents against Turkish rule, but died after contracting a fever. In 1825 the Turks defeated the Greeks and recaptured Missolonghi; the Greeks blew themselves up rather than surrender. (The independence of Greece was finally recognized in 1829.) In the painting, the woman personifying Greece, standing in front of a triumphant Turk, is at once classical allegory and real woman dressed in national costume. Delacroix has adapted classical conventions to his own requirements. The same adaptation occurs in *Liberty Leading the People*, in which the allegorical heroine leads the masses in the 1830 revolution discussed below.

The spirit of rebelliousness was expressed in the name of modernity, the thirst for which had originated in the Enlightenment but gathered in intensity during the Romantic era. You have already seen in Block 2, Units 7–8 how Stendhal's admiration for Napoleon was based on his status as a *modern* hero and genius. At this time, the notion of modernity carried with it a complex set of associations. To Stendhal and others, part of Napoleon's modernity derived from his allegiance to enlightened ideals: the Enlightenment had swept away the superstitions of the old order and there was something quite obviously heroic and reformist about the emperor's supposed allegiance to it. On the other hand, in literary and artistic matters the traditions of the Enlightenment were deemed to be too restrictive. In his 1823 pamphlet, *Racine and Shakespeare*, Stendhal prefers Shakespeare to Racine because he adopted a freer attitude towards subject matter and composition. He wants 'a language to suit the children of the Revolution': art accessible and relevant to his own time. This might be an uncomfortable process: 'It takes courage to be romantic, because you must take risks' (quoted in Brookner, 1971, p.48). To artists like Delacroix, modernity was associated, as in Stendhal's writings, with a rejection of servile imitation of a restricted classicism and with a search for art of contemporary relevance. You have already seen in Block 6, Units 24–25 the importance to Romantic artists of responding authentically to their own time. For example, Delacroix greatly admired the composer Rossini, who seemed to speak to his contemporaries' sensibility. But there was less positive, cheerful energy and heroism in Delacroix's *Chios* and *Sardanapalus* than Stendhal would have liked and than he expressed in his own novels. The two men remained firm friends, but on the basis that their modernizing spirit pulled them in slightly different directions. For Delacroix was not an uncompromising modernizer. He was suspicious of scientists and, like Wordsworth, regretted the impact on modern life of the railways. His modernity lay in the dark abysses of the Gothic.

Between 1826 and 1828, after seeing in London a dramatic adaptation of Goethe's play, Delacroix made a series of 18 lithographs of *Faust* (Plates 32.29–32.34 in the Illustrations Book are reproductions of six of these). A mixture of the comic and evil, these lithographs encapsulate both the sublime and Hugo's grotesque. They are peopled by strange, elongated figures, whose features have been described as 'mantis-like'; they have 'overt ball-and-socket jointing for elbows and knees' and are dressed in sixteenth-century style, in 'scaly, spiky costumes that seem to have a life independent of their wearers' (Joannides, 2001, p.142). This 'satanic' style (to use Stendhal's term) was drawn partly from prints of sixteenth-century Northern artists. The bodies of these insect-like figures express perfectly their moral qualities. Goethe said that in the lithographs Delacroix had surpassed the writer's own vision. But in spite of a contemporary fashion for the Gothic and the series' use of medieval settings, it did not sell well. Like *Sardanapalus*, it earned Delacroix many insults – including that of belonging to the 'school of the ugly'. Meanwhile, alongside *Sardanapalus* at the Salon of 1827–8, Delacroix exhibited a painting entitled *Mephistopheles appears before Faust* (see Plate 32.35). Of a more orderly composition, it nevertheless resembles *Sardanapalus* in its opulent red and gold colour scheme and in its references to evil and death. The antithesis of ideal classical beauty and of a didactic academic tradition, the *Faust* series of lithographs expresses the far reaches of Delacroix's modernity. Indeed, the ghosts, devils, skulls, monsters and galloping horses in the lithographs and in the painting synthesize and express the total liberation of his imagination.

It is important to place Delacroix's modernity in its historical context because it had, in its time, a political resonance. Delacroix was not exactly anti-establishment. He appreciated very much the government commissions he received in the 1820s and was relieved to find that, in the longer term, the fuss over *Sardanapalus* had not damaged his ability to attract further commissions. But his sympathies did lie with the Liberals of his age. You may recall from Block 2, Units 7–8 that in 1815, after the battle of Waterloo, the French monarchy was restored and Louis XVIII came to the throne. His rule was relatively benign. Initially he had to deal with opposition from both republicans and (Liberal, anti-monarchy) Bonapartists, as well as the continuing presence in Paris of the foreign troops who had helped to restore the monarchy. He brought stability to the country and its food supply, reorganized its finances and paid off its war debts. He also liberalized electoral and censorship laws. Throughout his reign, however, Louis faced fierce opposition from the right, known as the Ultras. This group supported the bid for power of the king's younger brother, Charles, Comte d'Artois, as well as seeking the restoration of the *ancien régime* privileges of the aristocracy and clergy. When Louis XVIII died in 1824 he was succeeded by this rival, who was crowned as Charles X. Charles's rule was marked by its significant protection of those landed nobles who had survived the Revolution, and of the clergy and the Catholic Church generally. Charles also dissolved the Chamber of Deputies and reintroduced stringent censorship laws. This sparked considerable Liberal opposition, as the Liberals championed the cause of constitutional government and meritocracy. In 1830 this conflict culminated in a further revolution, as a consequence of which the more liberally inclined Louis Philippe of the house of Bourbon-Orléans came to the throne. The uprising is captured in Delacroix's *Liberty Leading the People* (Plate 32.28 in the Illustrations Book), an innovative work in its heroic treatment of conventionally unheroic sections of society. The man on the left in the painting, carrying a sabre, is a factory worker; the man with a gun, next to him, is an artisan or foreman; the figure kneeling at Liberty's feet is a worker from the country, possibly a builder.

Delacroix made many satirical drawings that expressed his criticism of the monarchy (even its more liberal incarnation in the form of Louis XVIII), aristocracy and clergy, and that made clear his sympathies with Bonapartist Liberalism. Look again, for example, in the Illustrations Book at the Goya-esque Plate 32.25 (probably inspired by the anti-clerical satire in *Los Caprichos*) and Plate 32.26, and also look at Plate 32.36, *Acrobats' Riding Class* (1822). The latter depicts incompetent Ultra riders wearing ancient armour, clerical dress and *ancien régime* court attire. They fall off their horses as two demure figures look on from the middle. These are a Napoleonic cavalryman whose banner reads 'Glory, Honour, Fatherland', and a good bourgeois whose banner proclaims 'Fine Arts, Industry, Commerce, Talent and Virtues'. If Stendhal's modernity had found expression within the sphere of Napoleonic politics, Delacroix's defined itself in response to what he saw as the conservative, pro-classical and pro-monarchy academies[10] and those bourgeois who supported the reactionary Charles X. He abhorred their dislike of Voltaire and Rousseau, two of the Enlightenment's most eloquent critics of a corrupt monarchy, and found, in Stendhal and others, welcome exponents of a new aesthetic. Indeed *Sardanapalus*, with its defective ruler, has been interpreted as a 'grand moral fable meant to indict

[10] The French Royal Academy, abolished in 1793, had two years later become the National Institute of Sciences and Arts. In 1816 the separate schools of this institute, including what became the nineteenth-century Academy of Fine Arts, were restored to direct royal protection.

absolutism' (Athanassoglou-Kallmyer, 1991, p.111). Victor Hugo certainly perceived the relevance of the painting for the conservative contingent of the contemporary bourgeois establishment. His view (expressed in April 1828) summed up the archetypal Romantic reaction to bourgeois philistines:

> His *Sardanapalus* is a magnificent thing, and so gigantic that it is beyond small minds ... this beautiful work ... has not been successful with the bourgeois of Paris: *the jeers of fools form a fanfare for glory.*
>
> (Quoted in Johnson, 1981, p.120; trans. Walsh; italics in the original)

Critics of the painting, however, also included some Liberals who were alienated on aesthetic rather than political grounds (Lambertson, 2002, pp.79–85).

In the early years of the nineteenth century Romanticism experienced many subtle changes of direction. Stendhal admired the stoical heroism of David's paintings (see for instance Plate 32.5 in the Illustrations Book, *The Lictors returning to Brutus the Bodies of his Sons*), which became, for Delacroix, symbols of bourgeois reaction. With the constant call for innovation, rebellion and modernity came an ever-shifting set of priorities. Delacroix was not, by modern standards, radical in his politics. Later in his life, prompted by a further revolution in 1848 that brought about a republic in France, he said how much he disliked mass popular uprisings and regretted the destruction caused by the Revolution of 1789 His *Liberty Leading the People* had initially caused a stir because of its sympathetic and realistic treatment of the lower orders. Nevertheless, Delacroix won the cross of the Legion of Honour for this work and it was originally displayed in the Palais du Luxembourg, although it was taken down in 1832 as part of a conservative backlash against its vivid republican overtones. But the artist's later writings suggest that his principal allegiance was to the educated middle classes.

EXERCISE   Try to list as many features as you can of French Romantic art and artists, as explored here in section 3.

DISCUSSION
- The Romantic artist in the grip of genius and inspiration.

- The Romantic artist as one of an elite band of feeling souls, striving to communicate with others.

- A self-conscious approach to artistic creativity, individuality and identity.

- An acknowledgement that the true self and ultimate reality are concealed beneath a material, sensuous façade.

- A belief in a complex self accessible only to the initiated.

- A compulsion to rebel, innovate and modernize.

- A conscious abolition of traditional boundaries and categories of subject matter and genres.

- An attraction towards the Gothic, the fantastic and the irrational.

- An onslaught on conservatism, both cultural and political.

- A liberated use of the imagination.

Don't worry if you did not get all of these points, or if you listed or named them slightly differently. It is, in any case, difficult to define an approach to art that, in the case of Delacroix, consciously resisted all definition.

4   The Oriental and the exotic

At the end of this section you will be studying the material in Video 4, band 3, *Eugène Delacroix: The Moroccan Journey*. Before doing this, however, it will be useful to look at some of the factors that affected his treatment of the Oriental and the exotic in art. His choice of the Sardanapalus theme, for example, was probably the result of a complex web of cultural influences that acquired new significance in the context of French Romanticism. In many respects, Delacroix's conception of the Oriental had already been constructed for him by generations of French thinkers, writers, decorators and artists.

The interest of French writers in the Orient had been apparent since the seventeenth and early eighteenth centuries. Jean-Baptiste Tavernier (1605–89), for example, had explored Turkey, Persia and the Indies, while in 1711 Jean Chardin (1643–1713) had published in French his *Journey to Persia and the East Indies*. The work of explorers such as these had fuelled, in the eighteenth century, a strain of Orientalist literature that presented the East both as a world of sensuous delight and as an indirect critique of French society and government. Writers exploited a distancing, Oriental 'cover' in order to express ideas that would have offended government censors. Montesquieu's fictional *Persian Letters* (1721) used the device of two Persians visiting France and writing to those back at home in order to criticize French Catholicism, the French monarchy, aristocracy and social fashions. In 1748 Diderot's licentious novel, *Indiscreet Jewels*, based its narrative on Mangogul, sultan of the Congo, who, bored with life in his sumptuous palace, sets about amusing himself and his mistress Mirzoza by using a magic ring that makes all the 'jewels' (slang for vaginas) of the women associated with his court tell their individual stories. From these stories there emerges a rational critique of Catholic attitudes to sex and marriage that Diderot developed even further in his *Supplement to Bougainville's Voyage* (1772). In this work Diderot uses the travel accounts of the explorer Bougainville, who had visited Tahiti, to set out a case for more liberal attitudes to sexual relations than those supported by the Catholic Church and (superficially or officially) by his own society.

By the end of the eighteenth century enlightened rational critique played less of a role in Orientalist literature, which focused more on the Orient as a source of sensuous delight. Bernadin de Saint Pierre's *Paul and Virginie* (1788) revels in the perfume, shape and colour of the flora and fauna of Mauritius, where the novel's love story is based. Descriptions of the exotic environment are inextricably bound with those of the central couple's emotional states. This attention to visual intricacy, authenticating detail and local colour, primarily intended to delight and entertain the eye rather than to serve any obvious utilitarian function within a composition, is a later, less English manifestation of the picturesque you have already encountered in the works of William Gilpin. As you will remember from Block 4, Unit 16, Gilpin had himself inherited the term from even earlier French and Italian culture. Delacroix liked to incorporate intriguing details in many of his works, particularly sparkling costume details, although these were often painted loosely rather than precisely. When, in 1832, he travelled to Morocco, he described the country as 'picturesque' and devoted a great deal of time to recording the visual feast it offered. As you saw in Unit 31 on Brighton Pavilion, this concern with picturesque detail was nourished by a renewed scholarly interest in the East.

In the sphere of painting, decoration and architecture, you have already seen, in connection with the Royal Pavilion at Brighton, how Orientalist schemes of decoration, which were all the rage in the eighteenth century among those who sought a more colourful and sumptuous life, attained a particularly florid mode of expression in the early nineteenth century. This was a considerable development from the early Enlightenment Rococo, which had included Oriental subjects with graceful curves and conventional, theatre backdrop landscapes designed to complement elegant gold and white interior decoration heavily punctuated by mirrors and candlelight (see Plate 32.37 in the Illustrations Book, François Boucher's *Leopard Hunt*). **Turqueries** and chinoiseries had been extremely popular in furniture, wall decorations and ornaments (see Plates 32.38 and 32.39). The nineteenth century intensified the sensuous appeal of such effects. Delacroix himself observed and learned from Gros's Egyptian subjects, constructed from tradition and imagination rather than observation. He had also seen Islamic art objects – the Persian and Indian miniatures in the collection of his friend, the artist Jules-Robert Auguste.

In this context, we might see Delacroix's Sardanapalus as a modern Mangogul. He is idle, bored with his wealth, power and harem, but magnified by Romantic 'spleen' – unlike Mangogul, he is immersed in despair and tragic circumstances, and less amenable to being entertained. Delacroix was well read and Diderot was one of the authors he enjoyed, but it is significant that Sardanapalus, as Romantic sultan, lacks any association with Enlightenment wit and humour. His persona is inflected by the satanic aura of Byron's poetry or Goethe's *Faust* and, as we have seen, the abyss of hell beckons in the lower edge of Delacroix's painting. The hedonistic freedoms sought by the *philosophes* are here transformed into powers of darkness and evil.

The Oriental was often stereotyped by French writers and artists as the source of lustful pleasure that, in Catholic France, was forced to acquire the status of dream or fantasy. There was, for example, Christian suspicion (formally expressed by St John of Damascus) of the revelations that the prophet Mohammed claimed to have received in order to justify polygamy. There was also a prurient interest in the popular myth that he had decided to enclose his wives in a courtyard (the origin of the harem), and make them wear the veil, as the result of the suspected adultery of one of them, Aïsha. In the western mind, the harem figured alongside the Turkish bath as emblems of eastern sensuality. Islam had been characterized by the early Christians as a perversion, by the Arabs of the deserts, of Jewish and Christian beliefs. As you saw in your reading of Mungo Park's travels in Block 3, Units 12–13, a fear of Islam persisted in late eighteenth- and early nineteenth-century Europe, and this, along with Islam's mythical potential to express a suppressed western lasciviousness, meant that the Orient provided the perfect canvas on to which the Romantics could project their fears, longing and desire.

The sympathy of Byron, Delacroix and others for the Greeks, in their recent wars with the Turks, had become by 1824 a major concern of all European liberal opinion. This relates to a further Orientalist strand of thought inherited from the eighteenth century: the myth of the Turks as superstitious 'barbarians' and enemies of enlightened classical civilization. Although there had been political alliances between France and the Ottoman empire, there was a residual fear of 'Turks' and Moors generated by memories of their victories at Constantinople (1453), their occupation of Spain (up to the end of the fifteenth century) and a continuing awareness of their potential to seize power which was to persist into the twentieth century. You will recall from Block 2, Unit 9 how Napoleon's troops murdered thousands of Turks at Jaffa during his Egyptian or Middle Eastern campaign, allegedly as part of a 'civilizing mission'. This particular stereotype or caricature of the 'barbarian' came under strain in the Romantic era, however, as artists and writers appreciated the heroic skills of the Turks as warriors. For instance, in Delacroix's *Massacres of Chios* (Plate 9.2 in the Illustrations Book) the Turkish cavalryman in the foreground injects (Romantic) energy into an otherwise inert, dejected scene so that it is not clear whether our sympathies should lie with the passive Greek victims whose corpses or dying bodies litter the painting, or with the heroic but deviant Turkish aggressor who sweeps in from the right. It was also common, as you saw in Unit 9, to associate Oriental peoples with fatalism and passivity. *Massacres of Chios* played on these multiple associations. It spoke to contemporary fears of the overthrow of Christianity by Islam and of the total occupation of Greece (symbolic of civilized antiquity) by the invading barbarian. And yet it is the Turk in Delacroix's painting who seems to embody freedom and beauty by contrast with the diseased and (politically) oppressed bodies of the Greeks.

Napoleon himself shared these complex, ambivalent attitudes towards the Turks and Orientals. On the one hand, as he aspired to rival the accomplishments of Alexander the Great, he saw them as barbarians in need of civilizing influence; on the other, the Turks (and Islamic culture generally) were colourful and intriguing objects of imaginative fascination. We can see something of these changing, complex attitudes in another Orientalist painting completed by Delacroix, *The Combat of the Giaour and Hassan* (1826) (see Plate 32.40 in the Illustrations Book), one of several works on the same theme roughly contemporary with his other Byronic subject, *Sardanapalus*. The painting is based on Byron's poem, *The Giaour: A Fragment of a Turkish Tale* (1813). (Delacroix was as attracted to the poetry of Byron as he was to Goethe, and this attraction remained strong throughout his life.) In this heroic tale of late seventeenth-century Greece, a slave, Leila, flees the harem of a Turkish pasha (a high official of the Ottoman empire), Hassan. She goes to her Venetian warrior lover, the Giaour (a nickname given by Turks to non-Muslims), but is discovered, captured and thrown into the sea. The painting shows the Giaour seeking revenge: he ambushes Hassan and kills him in single combat. Hassan is both oppressive barbarian and energetic warrior, rushing towards us on his fiery steed. His exotic dress and flamboyant pose would have allowed western observers to flirt with notions of transgressive actions – that is, to abandon conventional boundaries of culture, gender and behaviour.

There was a similar ambivalence towards the Turks in music.[11] The plots of eighteenth-century 'Turkish' operas had represented Turks as both unenlightened barbarians and enlightened humanitarians. Rameau's *The Courtly Indies* (1735), for instance, encompasses four tales of love, the first of which, entitled *The Generous Turk*, is set in Turkey. It features a magnanimous pasha – a convention followed in two works both generally known as *The Unexpected Encounter*, Gluck's *La Rencontre imprévue* (1764) and Haydn's *L'Incontro improvviso* (1775), and by Mozart in *The Abduction from the Seraglio* (1782), among others. In the nineteenth century, however, Weber's one-act *Singspiel*[12] *Abu Hassan* (1811), which also has a Turkish setting, employed all-Turkish characters (instead of the European–Turkish encounters of the works previously

[11] I am grateful to Ross Winston for these details on the exotic in music.

[12] Spoken dialogue interspersed by song.

mentioned). 'Oriental' music was generally required to meet conventional expectations. Thus fashionable 'Turkish' instrumental music of the eighteenth century was represented orchestrally by triangle, cymbals and bass drum and by 'primitive' repeated chords. Throughout the arts, therefore, there was an attempt to recast Turkish identity in order to meet the needs of European cultural fashions.

As far as Delacroix's paintings are concerned, it is perhaps dangerous to associate them too closely with national stereotypes of any kind, since it has been pointed out that the way in which he represented 'racial' types was often driven by aesthetic concerns and traditions rather than by any real knowledge or observation (see Grimaldo Grigsby, 1999). Like many of his contemporaries, Delacroix blurred the distinctions between Turks, Moors, Arabs and Persians in his quest for a generalized 'Oriental', distinctive only in his or her difference from the European. The arbitrary approach to skin colour (the 'cadaverous tint') in paintings such as *Chios* stimulated among his critics fears of the 'racial' degeneration of the beloved Greeks of antiquity (Grimaldo Grigsby, 2002, pp.240–52), but could be explained by widespread confusion about 'racial' characteristics. The critics' preference for the traditional Hellenic beauty of the central figure in *Greece on the Ruins of Missolonghi* was telling: what mattered was allegiance to a specific, western ideal of beauty. There was an aesthetic hierarchy at play here that expressed, subliminally perhaps, western attitudes towards non-western cultures.

Heroic Byronic quests such as that of the Giaour were ideally suited to Delacroix's taste and formed part of his Romantic modernity. In the preface to his 1829 collection of poems, *The Orientals*, Victor Hugo describes Oriental themes as part of the rich tapestry of subject matter to be mined by Romantics. He suggests that literature should be like a medieval Spanish town that juxtaposes winding streets and Gothic cathedrals with the domes and partitions of a mosque – a graphic illustration of the crossing of aesthetic and cultural boundaries that have in common their opposition to the straight lines and order of the previously dominant neoclassical style.

The Oriental might be seen, then, as a convenient conduit for Delacroix's expressive genius. You may remember that he described inspiration as a 'slumbering lion, whose roarings stir your very being' (Pach, 1938, p.94). The combat of the Giaour, the drama and sumptuous frenzy of Sardanapalus's palace: these subjects fed his desire, as a Romantic, to escape imaginatively to a world more colourful and dramatic than that which he inhabited in reality. The exotic was, to late eighteenth- and early nineteenth-century thinkers and artists, the blatantly foreign, strange or unfamiliar. In his educational treatise *Émile* (1762) Rousseau, drawing on a gardening analogy, describes as 'exotic' that which is obviously opposed to the native, as he decries the bad effects wrought by society on nature and human nature: 'By human art is our native soil compelled to nourish exotic plants, and one tree to bear the fruits of another' (Eliot and Whitlock, 1992, vol.II, p.171).

The exotic is different or 'other'. By calling attention to its difference from the native or familiar, it gives us a clearer sense of our own identity or viewpoint. Similarly, Wordsworth criticized the 'profanation' of the native (Lakes) landscape resulting from the fashion for implanting exotic villas in prominent positions within the original wilderness (Anthology II, pp.100–4). And yet the exotic liberated the imagination, exuded energy and permitted the kinds of transgressive thinking favoured by many Romantics. The exotic has been defined by one scholar as 'the artistic exploration of territories and ages in which the free flights of imagination were possible because they lay outside the restrictive operation of classical rules' (Stevens, 1984, p.17). It was also associated with the opportunity to explore new cultures outside Europe and a host of novel picturesque details (*Le Robert*, 2000, vol.I, p.815). Essentially, it allowed westerners to explore their own cultural values and mindset in a way that has been seen by some commentators (for example, Said, 1991) as a kind of exploitative cultural imperialism that can undermine the possibility of assessing 'outsiders' on their own terms, of viewing things from their perspective or of being judged by them. These risks are seen to be greatest where the power politics of empire hold sway, but they can also be increased where a particular aesthetic dominates. Such was the case, perhaps, with the Romantic picturesque, which manipulated and exploited the Oriental for its purely visual potential and (western) appeal without penetrating its own values or perspectives.

It is significant that Delacroix characterized his genius as that of a wild animal, as the energy and exoticism of such creatures also inspired him as subjects. He went to see wild animals in the Jardin des Plantes, a botanical and zoological garden in Paris, and was fascinated by the large cats there (see Plate 32.41 in the Illustrations Book, *A Young Tiger playing with its Mother*). But, as with his Romantic predecessor Géricault, it was above all the horse that he used to express Romantic fury (see Plate 32.42, *Tiger attacking a Wild Horse*). The horse in *Sardanapalus* expresses a deep, sublime terror – a longstanding tradition in animal painting. In an earlier version of the animal combat theme by the English artist George Stubbs, for example (see Plate 32.43, *Horse attacked by a Lion*), the horse's expression derives from the 'catalogue' of facial expressions provided by the seventeenth-century French artist Charles Le Brun. Imbued with a capacity for human terror, this horse signifies the overwhelming impact of the sublime that was to form the focus of much Romantic creativity. Later in his career, after visiting Morocco, Delacroix sustained an interest in painting fiery Moorish horses in action (see Plate 32.44, *Lion Hunt*). These exotic horses and their riders are intended to express and intensify sublime wildness in a colourful idiom.

Recent commentators have read paintings such as *Sardanapalus* as revealing the personal character or values of the artist. Delacroix's recourse to the exotic and Oriental is seen as an extension of his obsession with his own desires. For example, Linda Nochlin (1983, pp.122–5) has interpreted this picture as an expression of masculine sadism; the cool, dandyish Sardanapalus being a surrogate for the artist himself, both creator and destroyer of all that is around him. To Nochlin, *Sardanapalus* signifies masculine fantasies about possessing, enjoying and destroying women's bodies. She argues that a specific historical context gave rise to such fantasies: Delacroix's ready access, as artist, to the female models he 'possessed' in his own studio. The Oriental setting of the painting defuses its sadistic charge by distancing the subject from nineteenth-century France. A similar point concerning male domination has been made (Grimaldo Grigsby, 2002, pp.255–6) concerning the depiction of women's bodies in *Chios,* particularly as Delacroix slept with the woman who modelled for the female corpse in the painting's foreground. Whether this was sadism, voyeurism or plain erotic fantasy, this artistic practice is related to the issue of the implied audience for the painting. Did Delacroix envisage a passive (male) viewer who was assumed to welcome such fantasies? It is true that he underestimated the general unease the work would create. The scholar Richard Wrigley has pointed out that the dominant official view of artists in restoration France was that of people 'properly unworldly – chaste, priest-like, a class apart from the rest of society' (Wrigley, 1993, p.135). This view was formed partly in order to counter the disruptive effects of the Revolution on the other-worldliness, spiritual and moral values that were felt to characterize the artist's studio in pre-revolutionary times. David's circle, for example, was thought to have become too much involved in politics. The restoration establishment perceived the proper artist as someone apart from the normal engagements of social life, debauchery or other worldly approaches. As we have seen, in some respects Delacroix, like many of the Romantics, intensified and celebrated this sense of a being apart from the 'common herd'. In other respects, however, his art engaged openly with sex, society and politics.

It is possible, then, to argue that Delacroix used Orientalism as a peg on which to hang his personal and Romantic obsessions and as a means of exploring and expressing his identity as an artist. There were, however, aspects of his approach to cultures outside Europe that suggested a less egocentric dimension. It is at this point that you should turn to Video 4, band 3 for an account of Delacroix's 1832 journey to Morocco. There, like others you have studied in the course (for example, Mungo Park and Byron), the artist developed his outlook and technique through travel. Turn now to your AV Notes for Video 4, band 3. These, and the video to which they relate, will introduce you to the particular circumstances of Delacroix's encounter with North Africa – an encounter that was to enable him to study another culture at close hand. Please work through the exercises in the AV Notes before returning to this unit.

5 Conclusion

Delacroix's fascination with the Oriental and the exotic both fuelled and influenced his Romantic tendencies. His journey to Morocco encouraged him to balance Romantic obsessiveness with classical restraint and to inject a significant degree of enlightened empirical observation into his art. He was seduced by the colour and the light of this foreign land, but his sensuous enjoyment of the picturesque developed alongside a scientific interest in colour and form. His responses to Morocco remained, however, deeply influenced by western cultural values.

This unit has tracked Delacroix's progression from an avid practitioner of a modified and modernized (Baroque) classicism to a professed, albeit somewhat reluctant, Romantic, and finally to a position (during his visit to Morocco) in which Romantic fantasy was infused by a dedication to first-hand observation and a new sense of living antiquity. In his *Death of Sardanapalus* he brought Romanticism to a dramatic climax. It was difficult for succeeding artists to surpass his achievements in creating bold and energetic fantasies. Nor could Delacroix sustain, within his own career, his earlier dedication to rebellion and innovation.

In the final years of his career Delacroix focused on monumental state commissions such as those for the church of Saint Sulpice and the Palais-Bourbon in Paris. He also continued to work on paintings inspired by his North African travels and wrote extensively on art. In 1857 he was elected a member of the Académie des Beaux-Arts. Fully integrated into the establishment, the reluctant Romantic rebel was eventually seen as the representative of an established aesthetic, Romantic classicism, that appeared outmoded by comparison with the modern, innovative realism of a new generation of artists such as Gustave Courbet (1819–77).

References

Athanassoglou-Kallmyer, N.M. (1991) *Eugène Delacroix: Prints, Politics and Satire 1814–1822*, New Haven and London, Yale University Press.

Brookner, A. (1971) *The Genius of the Future*, London and New York, Phaidon.

Brookner, A. (2000) *Romanticism and its Discontents*, London, Viking.

Carrington Shelton, A. (2000) 'Ingres versus Delacroix', *Art History*, vol.23, no.5, December, pp.726–42.

Eliot, S. and Whitlock, K. (eds) (1992) *The Enlightenment: Texts*, 2 vols, Milton Keynes, The Open University.

Gilpin, W. (1973) *Observations, Relative Chiefly to Picturesque Beauty, Made in the Year 1772, on Several Parts of England; Particularly the Mountains, and Lakes of Cumberland, and Westmoreland*, 2 vols, Richmond, Richmond Publishing Co. (first published 1786).

Goodman, J. (trans.) (1995) *Diderot on Art*, vol.1: *The Salon of 1765 and Notes on Painting*, New Haven and London, Yale University Press.

Gordon, G., Lord Byron (1970) *Byron: Poetical Works*, ed. F. Page, Oxford, Oxford University Press.

Grimaldo Grigsby, D. (1999) '"Whose colour was not black nor white nor grey, but an extraneous mixture, which no pen can trace, although perhaps the pencil may": Aspasie and Delacroix's *Massacres of Chios*', *Art History*, no.5, December, pp.676–704.

Grimaldo Grigsby, D. (2002) *Extremities: Painting Empire in Post-Revolutionary France*, New Haven and London, Yale University Press.

Hannoosh, M. (1995) *Painting and the 'Journal' of Eugène Delacroix*, Princeton, Princeton University Press.

Hugo, V. (1949) *Préface de Cromwell suivie d'extraits d'autres préfaces dramatiques*, Paris, Librairie Larousse (first published 1827).

Joannides, P. (2001) 'Delacroix and modern literature', in B.S. Wright (ed.) *The Cambridge Companion to Delacroix*, Cambridge, Cambridge University Press.

Jobert, B. (1998) *Delacroix*, Princeton, Princeton University Press.

Johnson, L. (1981) *The Paintings of Eugène Delacroix: A Critical Catalogue 1816–1831*, vol.1, Oxford, Clarendon Press.

Joubin, A. (ed.) (1996) *Delacroix: Journal 1822–1863*, Paris, Librairie Plon (first published 1931).

Lambertson, J.P. (2002) 'Delacroix's *Sardanapalus*, Champmartin's *Janissaries*, and Liberalism in the late restoration', *Oxford Art Journal*, vol.25, no.2, pp.65–86.

Nochlin, L. (1983) 'The imaginary Orient', *Art in America*, May, pp.119–37.

Pach, W. (ed. and trans.) (1938) *The Journal of Eugène Delacroix 1822–1863*, London, Jonathan Cape.

Le Robert dictionnaire historique de la langue française (2000) Paris, Le Robert.

Said, E.W. (1991) *Orientalism: Western Conceptions of the Orient*, Harmondsworth, Penguin (first published 1978).

Sewell, B. (2001) 'Masterpieces for 20 pence', *Evening Standard*, 26 January.

Spector, J.J. (1974) *Delacroix: The Death of Sardanapalus*, Harmondsworth, Penguin.

Spitzer, A. (2001) 'Delacroix in his generation', in B.S. Wright (ed.) *The Cambridge Companion to Delacroix*, Cambridge, Cambridge University Press.

Stevens, M.A. (ed.) (1984) *The Orientalists: Delacroix to Matisse, European Painters in North Africa and the Near East* (exhibition catalogue), London, Royal Academy.

Stewart, J. (ed. and trans.) (1971) *Eugène Delacroix: Selected Letters 1813–1863*, London, Eyre and Spottiswoode.

ten-Doesschate Chu, P. (2001) 'A science and an art all at once', in B.S. Wright (ed.) *The Cambridge Companion to Delacroix*, Cambridge, Cambridge University Press.

Vaughan, W. (1978) *Romanticism and Art*, London, Thames and Hudson.

Wilson-Smith, T. (1992) *Delacroix: A Life*, London, Constable.

Wright, B.S. (ed.) (2001) *The Cambridge Companion to Delacroix*, Cambridge, Cambridge University Press.

Wrigley, R. (1993) *The Origins of French Art Criticism: From the Ancien Régime to the Restoration*, Oxford, Clarendon Press.

Further reading

Delacroix, E. (2003) *The Journal of Eugène Delacroix*, trans. L. Norton, London, Phaidon (first published 1951). This is an accessible modern translation of Delacroix's journal entries from 1822 to 1863.

Jobert, B. (1998) *Delacroix*, Princeton, Princeton University Press.

Wheatcroft, A. (2003) *Infidels: The Conflict between Christendom and Islam 638–2002*, London, Viking. This book unravels the images and events that have influenced western perceptions of the East and touches on many events and artefacts central to A207, such as the Greek Wars of Independence (including Chios and Missolonghi), stereotypical western views of the Turks, Napoleonic Oriental paintings and Islamic North Africa.

Conclusion to Block 7

Prepared for the course team by Nicola J. Watson

In this block we have been looking at the development of a Romantic view of the East in the early years of the nineteenth century, at the aesthetic opportunities that the East offered to the arts as they were in transition from Enlightenment to Romantic values, and at the ways in which these opportunities are manifested in the Royal Pavilion at Brighton and in Delacroix's painting. We have told the story of two parallel metamorphoses: the Pavilion's transformation from neoclassical symmetries to Romantic fantasy; and Delacroix's uneasy translation of French classical traditions into a Romantic idiom and emphasis, becoming almost accidentally in the process a reluctant model of the 'Romantic artist'. Though the transition from the Enlightenment to the Romantic seems, with the benefit of hindsight, to be natural and inevitable, these two stories make clear the lurches, hesitations and scepticisms that accompanied the process – which should remind us that such changes are neither inevitable nor seamless, but accidental and patchy. We can also see from these two case studies how important the idea of the East was to emergent Romantic thought and imagination as an imaginary place of sensual freedom and ruthlessly individualistic social transgression. In the case of the Pavilion, we note a shift from a neoclassical aesthetic freighted with Enlightenment ideas of landed responsibility to a Romantic fantasy designed to dramatize one man's unique Romantic sensibility and sense of royal power. With Delacroix's experimental *The Death of Sardanapalus*, we see how an eastern subject licensed a swerve away from a 'responsible' art in the service of the high ideals of the state – marked as such by classical perspective, balanced composition, muted colouring and smooth surface – into the realms of fantasy, violence and Romantic self-expression. Both works import the monstrously violent into the domestic, and play with that excitement. Both are noticeably invested in the excessive and overwhelming, in disorientating shifts of perspective and scale, violent colour contrasts and dazzling surface effects, in the hybrid and the grotesque, the irrational and the irregular, in a wild exuberance of 'serpentine lines and dramatic diagonals ... strenuous movements towards and away from the spectator', and in dramatic lights and shadows (Sewell, 2001). They both aim to provoke a sort of delirium in their spectators. Both objects implicitly claim a Romantic exceptionality as the expressions of a force field of individual 'genius'. Although Delacroix supplies a theory of 'responsibility' in his writings about the function of the Romantic artist and Romantic art in relation to the viewer, and the Prince of Wales also seems to have had a sense of artistic responsibility as he acted as showman host to his guests, both works retain a strong flavour of the highly personal and self-dramatizing. As you have seen, it is possible to read Sardanapalus as a representation of Delacroix himself, and there is a flavour of Sardanapalus hanging around the figure of the Prince Regent, too. Both works have a complicated relation to the Romantic – they are consciously innovative but ambiguously Romantic. In the event the verdict of history was that *The Death of Sardanapalus was* Romantic but that the Pavilion *wasn't*, quite.

In many ways, this verdict depends on modern ideas that were crystallizing at the time about art, the artist and the audience. The Pavilion was a commissioned piece of art – commissioned, moreover, by royalty. Its architects were therefore in service to the monarchy rather than being entirely independent; equally, its artist was, arguably, the prince himself. The audience for the Pavilion was in the first instance provided by the prince as patron, and then by his intimates; and although (as we have seen) they were often highly critical in private of the prince's fantasy palace, there was no room allowed to them for the public expression of such reservations. Perhaps this, more than anything else, accounts for the sense of fatigue that many of the visitors expressed. The Pavilion, for all its modern investment in idiosyncrasy, thus expressed an older relation between art, artist and audience – the interconnections characteristic of court patronage. Of course, the wider public could and did criticize, but they were excluded from those all-important evening performances of royal taste and power for which the exteriors and interiors were merely the setting.

By contrast, *The Death of Sardanapalus* was displayed to a Salon audience as an artist's masterpiece. It was viewed as a polemic by an important, original and rebellious artist – a Romantic artist in his privileged access to the real – and as a statement that mediated and moralized the real to its audience. The Salon setting, moreover, allowed this Romantic fantasy to be viewed within an emphatically public sphere with well-established traditions of critical detachment.

Compared with the Royal Pavilion, Delacroix's painting is more Romantic aesthetically, delivering a larger dose of the inexplicit, the mysterious, the immaterial and the suggestive. It is more extreme in its exploration (perhaps even endorsement) of personal desire, less socialized, less domestic, more sexually explicit, more candidly violent, more downright debauched and more aggressively modern. Its pleasures, unlike the Pavilion's, were not policed by social restraints. On the other hand, and at the same time, the catastrophe portrayed has it both ways – indulging itself in a fantasy of glamorous self-damnation (think of Don Giovanni) *and* soliciting a reading of itself as critical of Sardanapalus's self-indulgence. Thus the painting can also be read as supplying a vivid indictment of a world-weary, defeated, egotistical sensualist, a fiction of the downfall of absolutism, and a critical exploration of the effects of unleashing personal desire and giving rein above all to self-expression. *The Death of Sardanapalus* thus expresses *and* critiques the urges that drive the Romantic. The painting marks a dynamic paralysis, a fierce desire for trangression countered by its equally dramatic frustration.

If this paralysis is typically Romantic, it may be traceable to post-Napoleonic politics: it does not do to forget that both the Prince Regent and Delacroix, in their different ways, found themselves in peculiarly ambiguous positions vis-à-vis royal power. One saw his power deferred again and again, and only finally achieved it in the context of well-founded new fears of revolution. The other found himself, post-Waterloo, a newly fledged and not entirely convinced royalist. Perhaps it is not surprising that both of them were interested in fictions of royal power, and that both were obliged none the less to make these fictions 'foreign' or exotic.

Reference

Sewell, B. (2001) 'Masterpieces for 20 pence', *Evening Standard*, 26 January.

Glossary

Unit 31

Chinoiserie: the deployment of 'Chinese' motifs within interior decor, popular from the early eighteenth century onwards. The most widespread example of this is the so-called 'willow pattern' used on domestic china which persists to this day.

Clerestory: an upper part of a wall carried on arcades, and pierced with windows to allow light to penetrate.

Coffering: deep panels sunk into a domed ceiling.

Cornice: a crowning moulding projecting horizontally at the junction of a wall and ceiling.

Cove/Coving: a surface of concave form linking wall and ceiling.

Cupola: a diminutive domed form, visible above a roof.

Enfilade: a French term, signifying the alignment of all the doorways in a suite of rooms so as to create a vista when the doors are open, thus avoiding corridors. The word is also used to denote the alignment of mirrors in such a way as to create a similar set of vistas.

Fan-vaulting: inverted half-cones or funnel shapes with concave sides. The style was originally designed to form a vaulted roof in late **Perpendicular** church architecture, but by the late eighteenth century it was used for decoration only.

Fretwork: the practice of piercing thin sheets of wood with cut-out patterns. In the Royal Pavilion, much of this is actually executed in *trompe l'oeil* style painting and is 'Chinese' in its straight-sided shapes.

Gothick: (spelled with a 'k' to distinguish it from true Gothic, a medieval style of church architecture, and from the Victorian Gothic Revival) an eighteenth-century English style based only vaguely on archaeologically correct Gothic, with a pronounced taste for the exotic, especially **chinoiserie**, and so connected with Rococo frivolity and, latterly, with the picturesque.

Grotesque: derived from the ornamentation in ancient Roman grottoes discovered during the Renaissance, in the eighteenth century this term came to be applied to decorative motifs of all kinds of Roman origin, including those used in elegant, neoclassical interiors. In the Romantic era the term acquired darker meanings and was used by Victor Hugo to suggest strange and disturbing mixtures of the comic and the tragic, the satanic and the farcical. Generally, the 'grotesque' satisfied a Romantic thirst for intense sensory and emotional stimulation.

Minaret: a tall slender tower (circular, rectangular or, as in the Brighton Pavilion, polygonal) associated with mosques.

Mog(h)ul: a term used by contemporaries to refer to Indian Muslim culture.

Parapet: a low wall at the edge of a roof, which may be ornamented, pierced with holes or left plain.

Perpendicular: a term used to identify church architecture from the beginning of the fourteenth century. It is characterized by particularly elongated forms, e.g. spires.

Reticulation: arranged to look like a net, with the same figure repeated all over the surface.

Rotunda: a building or part of a building shaped like a cylinder both inside and outside, especially one covered with a dome.

Spandrel: a triangular plane between two arches.

Strawberry Hill Gothick: this term, derived from Horace Walpole's fantasy home at Strawberry Hill, signifies a violently exaggerated and delicate mock **Gothick** style.

Taste: a key eighteenth-century term, on which whole books have been written. Broadly speaking, however, to possess a correct taste and the financial means of deploying and displaying it denoted high social status. This was usually, although not always, associated with landed or 'old' wealth rather than with 'new' wealth.

Trompe l'oeil: from the French, meaning literally 'to trick the eye' – i.e. to trick it into seeing something that is not there. The term is used of a painting technique which deceives the eye into thinking that a two-dimensional image of something (for example, a tassel or a vase) is the thing itself.

Unit 32

Classical style: derived from antique art, architecture and statuary, the classical style conveyed to the eighteenth century via the Renaissance was characterized by rationalism and idealism. It was infused by a sense of legible structure, order and harmony. In painting, this meant the use of a clearly legible picture space, arranged hierarchically around the central figure or motif (in history painting, a 'hero' perhaps; in landscape a prominent motif in the middle distance). Figure groupings were organized into stable (for example, pyramidal) geometric formations and were balanced across the canvas. Light and shade were used to highlight or unify pictorial elements rather than to dazzle, dapple or call attention to themselves. There were different modes of the classical style, principally the Baroque and the **neoclassical**.

Distemper: a water-based paint mixed with glue (to make it adhere to the canvas) and with chalk (to make it fill in the pores of the ground or canvas to which it is to be applied).

Gothic novel: a particularly sensational variant of romance literature, popular in the late eighteenth and early nineteenth centuries, that focused on horror and irrational passion. Delacroix had read works by such accomplished writers in the genre as Ann Radcliffe (1764–1823) and Mathew Lewis (1775–1818). His own early Gothic writings included *Alfred* and *The Dangers of Court*. Usually inspired by the darkness of Gothic or medieval architecture and social practices, this type of writing often focused on priests or nobles who abused the young and innocent and used castles and monasteries as settings.

Lay-in: the application of a layer of neutral colour (such as **distemper**) to serve as underpainting. It could be lightened or darkened in order to set the tonal pattern of the painting.

Neoclassical style: a style of painting made famous by Jacques-Louis David and his followers. It was characterized by a stark linearity, austere settings, geometrically planned compositions that often made use of horizontal, frieze-like arrangements of figures, and legible use of picture space. (The term 'Neoclassicism' is also sometimes more loosely used to denote the much broader phenomenon of the revival of interest in antiquity evident in eighteenth- and early nineteenth-century art and architecture – see also the Glossary to Blocks 2 and 5.)

Planimetric composition: a type of pictorial composition, typical of **neoclassical style**, that is structured around an implied grid of horizontal and vertical planes or layers. If we imagine the illusory space of a painting as a cube, then that cube can be divided into horizontal and vertical planes or 'slices' along sets of parallel lines. (The vertical planes might be compared to a series of theatre backdrops running in parallel into the depth of the stage space.) Objects and figures are arranged along these lines so that the total effect is one of balance and stability. Horizontal arrangements of figures along a specific vertical plane were particularly characteristic of the neoclassical.

Turquerie: the use of 'Turkish' motifs and sources of inspiration for interior decor and ornamentation, which was popular in the early nineteenth century.

Course Conclusion: An Overview of Romanticism

Prepared for the course team by Linda Walsh and Antony Lentin

Contents

There are no additional study components to the Course Conclusion.

Objectives

The aim of the Course Conclusion is to help you to draw together some of the strands of the course and to review various ways in which the texts you have studied demonstrate a shift towards Romanticism. After studying this Conclusion you should be able:

- to identify the main characteristics of Romanticism;
- to reflect on some of the ways in which cultural shifts discussed in the Course Introduction relate to the texts you have studied;
- to appreciate some of the differences between Enlightenment and Romanticism;
- to demonstrate some appreciation of the complex nature of cultural change.

1   Reviewing cultural trends

EXERCISE   Look back now at pp.60–1 of the Course Introduction (Unit 1), where a list is set out summarizing some of the main cultural shifts in the period *c.*1780–1830. If, as suggested there, you have made notes under the relevant headings, you should be well placed to comment on the strengths and weaknesses of the kinds of general statement made in the Introduction. Let us take point no. 15, where one suggested characteristic of the shift to Romanticism is a 'growing consciousness of the political influence and cultural identities of the people/working classes'. This shift relates perhaps to part of the 'context', rather than the 'essence', of the rise of Romanticism, but the two ideas are integrally related. How adequate do you feel this summary point is?

DISCUSSION   To some extent, of course, your answer to this question will depend on the texts you have studied most thoroughly or remembered most vividly. It may be, for instance, that in tracking examples of an awareness of the specific cultural identity of 'the people' you noted the way in which John Newton and William Cowper adapted religious worship to their needs through the *Olney Hymns*; or Robert Owen's attempts to address the social needs of factory workers; or perhaps the growing awareness of the conditions and needs of the new mass armies conscripted by the French state in the revolutionary and Napoleonic wars (in Audio 3, tracks 8–12, *Images of Napoleon*, evidence is cited of Napoleon's accessibility to his troops and his concern for their welfare); or the plight of the Spanish people and guerrilla 'freedom fighters' in their resistance to the French portrayed in such works as Goya's *Disasters of War*. All of these sources may indicate an awareness of a working people's culture that can be distinguished from the culture of other (dominant) sections of society or from a broader national culture. In looking for examples of a growing consciousness of the political influence of the people, you might have thought of the exaltation of the *sans-culottes* evident in Boilly's portrait (Plate 6.1 in the Illustrations Book); or possibly of the fact that Delacroix's *Liberty Leading the People* includes representatives of some of the 'lower' sections of society.

All these sources might suggest significant efforts to understand and express the political force, culture and social needs of the common people. And yet there are substantial counter-examples. Think, for instance, about the ultimate social effects of the Revolution and the Napoleonic era, which reflected above all the triumph and cultural preferences of the middle and upper echelons of society and brought greater status to the tastes of capitalist 'new money'. Think too about the role of the lower orders in a work such as *Faust*: are there any real signs here that the common people are moving centre-stage, or are they reduced to stock dramatic characters? In this period we can perhaps see the beginnings of a new self-consciousness among ordinary people and an incipient sense of a widening circle of political liberty, but (with the possible exception of documents relating to certain stages in the Revolution) we still seem a long way off from a democratic ethos in the wider culture of nineteenth-century Europe.

You have probably begun to appreciate just how complex a picture emerges from immersion in the texts and artefacts produced during a specific historical period, especially one so full of change as the half-century 1780–1830. For a thorough analysis of the key trends identified in the Course Introduction, it would be necessary to read much more widely and reflect more deeply than a single course allows. A different selection of texts, for example, might suggest different conclusions. There remains, however, considerable merit in sketching out a large picture, to be reworked and completed as further evidence emerges. In the remainder of this Conclusion we shall outline the main characteristics of Romanticism as suggested by the evidence of many of the texts you have studied, and (as in the Course Introduction) we shall, where relevant, occasionally refer briefly to other people, events and trends from the period under study that do not form part of the course. As we proceed, we shall pause from time to time to consider the strength and relevance of some of the key trends identified in the Course Introduction.

2   Romanticism

'I must ... protest against the notion that Romanticism can be enclosed within a concept; for Romantic precisely means that it oversteps all bounds,' wrote the Danish philosopher Søren Kierkegaard in 1836 (quoted in Thorlby, 1966, p.146). His remark underlines the fact that while the main characteristics of the Enlightenment can be delineated with reasonable clarity, there is less agreement about defining the Romanticism that dominated the early decades of the nineteenth century. As with the Enlightenment, there were national varieties of Romanticism, German as well as English, which are distinguishable both from each other and from French Romanticism. But German, English and French Romanticism also influenced one another as well as influencing developments in countries such as Russia, Italy, Poland and Spain. There was a general cultural cross-fertilization, which enables us to draw some broad conclusions about the common characteristics of European Romanticism.

The term 'Romanticism' can be applied in any or all of the following ways:

- to a period (roughly the first four decades of the nineteenth century, but often also the end of the eighteenth century);
- to styles, or modes of expression, that challenged the predominant classicism of the eighteenth century in literature, art, architecture and music;
- to a set of shared values distinguishable from those of the Enlightenment.

You will have found all these usages in this course. Like the *philosophes* of the Enlightenment, Romantic thinkers were conscious of belonging to a new movement of ideas; and just as in the eighteenth century there were various ways of describing oneself as 'enlightened', so 'Romantic' was a term used self-consciously from the early nineteenth century onwards in order to identify a variety of allegiances.

Despite the difficulties of summarizing the central qualities of this heterogeneous culture, it is generally accepted that the following characteristics came into prominence in European Romanticism:

- an emphasis on feeling and impulse;
- a focus on self-expression, introspection and self-discovery;
- an attraction to the mysterious, the spiritual, the obscure and the unknown;
- a recognition of nature as an autonomous, dynamic and self-transforming force;
- a recognition of the uniqueness of the individual, an exalted concept of the hero and of the exceptionality of the 'genius' as someone above and beyond the normal rules of art, conduct or ethics as understood in the Enlightenment;
- a sense of loss and melancholic inadequacy in the face of the sublime;
- the conclusion that the quest for objective truth may be an illusion.

Many of these trends and attitudes were identified in the list in the Course Introduction. Not all of them are present in any one 'Romantic' text. Nor should it be supposed that every creative artist and thinker in the period thought of himself or herself as a Romantic or that all their counterparts in the eighteenth century subscribed to the principles of the Enlightenment. Jane Austen (1775–1817), whose novels appeared in the centre of our period, had more in common with Dr Johnson than with Byron. Nevertheless, to judge from the evidence of most of the texts used for this course, it seems fair to speak of an overall Enlightenment culture and way of thinking that was dominant in Europe until at least the time of the French Revolution, and which gradually gave way to attitudes and modes of expression that we call Romantic. And you can see from the texts you have studied how dramatically different the Romantic mindset was from that of the Enlightenment. Let's re-examine briefly some of the key aspects of Romanticism that have surfaced in the texts.

Romantic feeling, humanitarianism and national consciousness

Broadly speaking, the Enlightenment outlook was characterized by reason, the Romantic mindset by feeling. This generalization is obviously crude: to depict Voltaire, Diderot or Dr Johnson as somehow devoid of emotion would be to ignore their human traits, their powerful personalities and their passionate attachment to particular causes. Hume himself argued that reason is 'the slave of the passions' – that is, the primary motivating force in human action is emotion, and the principal role of reason is to work out the means by which to achieve the goals dictated to us by our emotions. Mozart's Don Giovanni is among the fictitious characters who yields without a second thought to the promptings of emotion and impulse: a balanced, prudent Humean alliance of reason and passion does not suit this hero! It would, of course, be equally wrong to suggest that all Romantics were constantly a prey to anarchic emotionalism. The distinction is often a question of degree and balance. The Enlightenment insisted on imposing rational control upon feeling, so that when we study Mozart and Hume, for example, and even perhaps Rousseau and the Marquis de Sade, what emerges at least in some degree are such common characteristics as order, discipline and rationality. Increasing respect for and indulgence in feeling was one of the indicators that the Enlightenment was giving way to Romanticism. The distinction is probably more stark in the texts produced towards the end of our period than in the earlier texts, though no doubt you detected in Rousseau the early manifestations of this shift in emphasis. One of the key manifestations of the shift was the way in which a marked taste for classical order and restraint gave way to sources of inspiration drawn from religion, the supernatural and the Gothic.

Like Rousseau, William Wilberforce felt that intellectual understanding alone was inadequate to human needs and ignored the spiritual side of human nature. In his view, religious understanding and worship ought to be enriched by direct personal engagement and an outpouring of warm, spontaneous feelings. This propensity for a deeper, more personal piety, derived from seventeenth-century Puritanism, was also prevalent in German Pietism, a variant of German Protestantism influential in the eighteenth and nineteenth centuries that inspired many Romantics, such as the artist Caspar David Friedrich (1774–1840), whose work you encountered in Block 6, Units 24–25. Pietism, as you saw in Block 3, Unit 10, was also arguably an important source of Anglo-American Evangelicalism. Meanwhile, a religious revival in France was signified by Napoleon's Concordat of 1802, whereby he made temporary peace with

Pope Pius VII and restored the Catholic Church to a position of spiritual authority in France throughout the nineteenth century. Napoleon's motives were grounded in reasons of state, but the Concordat also corresponded to a genuine mood in French society. It coincided with the appearance of *Le Génie du christianisme* (*The Genius of Christianity*, 1802) by François-René de Chateaubriand (1768–1848). This eloquent and immensely popular book was an apologia for the restoration of religion as a necessary supplement to human wants, a call to draw together social bonds and to reconcile past and present through allegiance to a living Church with an age-old history and tradition. It appeared at the right moment, as a kind of antidote to the anti-clerical and anti-religious dimension of the Enlightenment temper, which was usually critical or ironic, and sometimes strident. In France and England this negative approach to religion now seemed to many to be facile, arid, emotionally sterile and unrewarding, and, given the experience of the French Revolution, socially divisive and dangerous. The poet and artist William Blake (1757–1827), who held to a mystical form of Christianity, upheld the higher wisdom of the spiritual:

> Mock on mock on, Voltaire Rousseau
> Mock on mock on! 'Tis all in vain!
> You throw the sand against the wind
> And the wind blows it back again.

> (Blake, 1982, p.477)

You may feel that Rousseau was a less accurate target than Voltaire in Blake's attack on eighteenth-century anti-clericalism, but the quotation illustrates the poet's reaction to this central aspect of the French Enlightenment.

Pope Pius himself, who suffered years of imprisonment at Napoleon's order and bore his ordeal with saintly resignation, did much to restore the appeal of Catholicism in Europe. Chateaubriand's nostalgic appeal (like Friedrich's) to the romance of the Middle Ages, cathedrals, the Gothic and the spiritual – in stark contrast to the Enlightenment's aversion to all such manifestations of the 'Dark Ages' – also offered, to Catholics, Protestants, Russian Orthodox and non-believers alike, what proved a highly popular aesthetic alternative to the domination of the classics. A key work of Romanticism was Madame de Staël's *De l'Allemagne* (*On Germany*, which first appeared in England in 1813, having been banned by Napoleon), in which Staël contrasts the lure of the north, the knightly and the Christian with the prevalent Roman-style classicism of Napoleonic France. Staël, as we have seen, was a notable representative of the emerging female voice in public culture.

The realm of religion was one in which the expression of emotion had always perhaps (with the exception of mainstream Anglicanism) received more respect compared with other areas of life. Think, for example, of Handel's *Messiah* (1741), Haydn's *Creation* (1798), or Mozart's *Requiem*

(1791). The achievement of Romanticism was to disseminate this quest for emotional intensity into areas of enquiry and activity other than religion. Thus Goethe's Faust seeks experience more intense than that attainable through the intellect alone and the search for empirical knowledge, even if this means entering into a cycle of striving and despair. Schubert wrote songs that express grief, loss, defiance, intense happiness, horror and solitary reflection. Byron's *Childe Harold's Pilgrimage* evokes emotions of guilt, ruin, alienation and loss in signalling the extraordinary sensibility of its hero and establishing a highly emotional relationship with the reader. This deep capacity for feeling was often pursued for its own sake and at its worst verged on sentimentality (the affectation of emotions not genuinely felt). It was also associated at times with the expression of a humanitarian impulse. Many Romantics wanted to share imaginatively (if not always practically) in the plight of the poor and oppressed. In his poems Wordsworth empathizes with the cold, starving beggars and shepherds of the Lakeland fells in a way that was typical of the new sensitivity to *feeling* of all kinds, including suffering. This broad humanitarianism also made its presence felt in larger public contexts such as that of the Royal Institution, which tried to apply science to the improvement of the lot of the poor through, for example, the development of agricultural technology. It helped to ensure that the Enlightenment's concern with social reform persisted into the nineteenth century.

Europe's most influential promoter of the cult of the Middle Ages, of knights in armour, crusaders and courtly chivalry, was the poet and novelist Sir Walter Scott. Scott also brought out something else of great and growing significance in the nineteenth century and beyond: a connection between natural scenery, the historic environment and *national self-consciousness*. Unalloyed national feeling was something which had held little appeal for the *philosophes*. They, you will recall, prided themselves on being members of an intellectual elite, a cosmopolitan fraternity of like-minded men across the Continent, a kind of European freemasonry (and many leading men throughout our period, including Mozart, Sade, Goethe, Napoleon, Scott, Schubert, Stendhal, Soane and the Prince Regent, were indeed freemasons). The language, literature and culture of France formed the common background of the Enlightenment, and the assumption that Paris was the intellectual and cultural centre of Europe continued into the Revolution and the Napoleonic era. During the Revolution, the National Convention (France's representative assembly) conferred the highest honour it could conceive of in bestowing French citizenship, honorary membership of *la grande nation* (the great nation), on selected individuals from America, Britain, Germany and elsewhere, who were thus distinguished for their services to 'humanity'. But the revolutionary and Napoleonic wars also stimulated the opposite feelings of attachment to particular national landscapes:

O Caledonia! Stern and wild,
Meet nurse for a poetic child!
Land of brown heath and shaggy wood,
Land of the mountain and the flood,
Land of my sires! what mortal hand
Can e'er untie the filial band
That knits me to thy rugged strand!

(Scott, *The Lay of the Last Minstrel*, Canto 6, 1805; Gardner, 1991, p.519)

Note Scott's suggestion here that the poet is particularly susceptible to national feeling, and the implicit approval given to such feeling as basic and natural. Scott's influence on Romanticism as poet and historical novelist can hardly be overemphasized. Turning away from the characteristic Enlightenment concern with a generalized concept of 'humankind', 'human nature' and the measurable progress of civilization celebrated by Voltaire and Condorcet, Scott focused sympathetically on the particular, the individual culture, the moment in history, the actual environment, its local colour, its organic growth from national roots. He fostered a particular pride in the history, culture and landscape of his own country, Scotland. In the Course Introduction (pp.36–7) we dwelt briefly on Dr Johnson's rather unsympathetic but highly rational Enlightenment perspective on the Scottish Highlands in his *Journey to the Western Isles of Scotland* (1775). With still greater condescension, Edward Gibbon, in the first volume of *The Decline and Fall of the Roman Empire* (1776), explained why in his view the Romans did not conquer Scotland:

> The masters of the fairest and most wealthy climates of the globe turned with contempt from gloomy hills assailed by the winter tempest, from lakes concealed in a blue mist, and from cold and lonely heaths, over which the deer of the forest were chased by a troop of naked barbarians.

(Gibbon, 1998, p.7)

Half a century after Johnson's and Gibbon's disparaging dismissals, Scott's celebration of the uniqueness of the Scottish landscape, history and culture was signalled in 1822 when George IV, having bestowed a baronetcy on the writer, paid a state visit to Scotland – and even wore a kilt for the occasion.

While *philosophes* in every capital from Madrid to Moscow had prided themselves on their affinity with a French-speaking cultural elite radiating out from Paris, what interested many Romantic writers and artists were precisely those features that distinguished their people from the French super-culture and made them nations in their own right: their geography, scenery, vernacular language, customs, folklore, faith. In Germany such national roots were researched by the Brothers Grimm in their *Children's and Domestic Tales* (1812–22; the so-called 'Fairy Tales'), *German Legends* (1816–18) and *German Grammar* (1819–37). Mme de Staël's *On*

Germany, banned by Napoleon as 'un-French' (see Block 2), was hugely influential in introducing Germany, German culture and German Romanticism to the wider European public, running to six editions between 1814 and 1819. It was to German roots, to myth, folktale and superstition, that Goethe turned in parts of *Faust* and in his fantastic poem of the sinister force in the wood, 'Der Erl-König', evocatively set to music by Schubert in a manner very different from that of Mozart. Meanwhile, the reactionary philosopher Joseph De Maistre (1753–1821) turned his back on a fundamental Enlightenment postulate when he wrote: 'In the course of my life I have seen Frenchmen, Italians, Russians, etc. ...; but *Man* I have never met. If he exists, it is contrary to my knowledge' (quoted in Thorlby, 1966, p.145).

The experience of the Napoleonic Wars intensified this cult of national awareness. Resistance to the French sometimes transformed patriotism from its eighteenth-century classical sense of civic-mindedness and public spirit into a mystical exaltation of national solidarity, a sublimation of individuality into a collective enthusiasm remote from the cosmopolitanism of the *philosophes*. Resistance to Napoleon in French-occupied Germany became a 'War of Liberation', a national crusade. The patriotic poet Ernst Moritz Arndt (1769–1860) declared that 'in this exalted human feeling ... I am no longer a sinful and suffering man, I am at one with the *Volk* [nation] and with God' (quoted in Hampson, 1968, p.192). Arndt's 'Lieder für Teutsche' ('Songs for Germans', 1813) included the popular poems 'Vaterlandslied' ('Song of the Fatherland') and 'Was ist das Deutsche Vaterland?' ('What is the German Fatherland?'). In 'Vaterlandslied', Arndt called on Germans to take up arms in a 'holy war':

> Let drums and flutes along our way
> Ring out our battle-cry;
> We all are eager, man for man,
> Today to do or die;
> Our swords to stain with hangman's blood,
> With foeman's blood to drench;
> A sweet revenge to Germans all,
> The day we slay the French!

(Langenbucher, 1937, p.166; trans. Lentin)

EXERCISE   Which cultural changes or trends have been identified in this section of the Course Conclusion?

DISCUSSION   A growing emphasis on feeling; a movement away from classical and rational constraints; a growing emphasis on national consciousness.

We can see from the discussion in this section how the weight placed by the Enlightenment on the discovery of rational, universal truths applicable to all of humankind came under fire as the cultural and political climate fostered a new emphasis on the emotions and on individual and national self-consciousness. But how solid are these generalizations? When considering, for example, the suggestions that emotion grew in importance and that there was a move away from classical restraints, think of the persistence of artists such as Delacroix in modifying rather than rejecting the classical tradition, and of his insistence on careful preparatory work for his paintings alongside the use of rapid, inspirational sketches. And how was Byron able to write letters about the practical details of his travels while apparently consumed by Romantic malaise in the poetry he was writing? Did reason and practicality persist as important modes of behaviour? As for national self-consciousness, Goethe was never attracted by the drums-and-trumpets nationalism of Arndt, and continued to pay tribute to French culture and to work towards a German contribution to what he called 'world literature'. Be prepared to challenge, nuance and refine generalizations.

Romanticism and nature

While the Enlightenment regarded nature as an object of study and a resource to be understood and controlled for people's benefit and pleasure (think of the varieties of eighteenth-century landscape garden), the Romantics, inspired perhaps by Rousseau and by those strains of Enlightenment thought that had promoted nature as the source of ideal solutions to society's ills, regarded it as a source of power, wisdom and knowledge *in its own right*. The power of nature as a self-generating force had been postulated by materialist thinkers such as Diderot, who visualized the ability of matter to generate life and transform species spontaneously without the guiding hand of God. Goethe too, who was also known for his scientific researches, saw nature as a dynamic, organic force, though his view of its relationship to the divine was very different from Diderot's. Goethe encapsulated the fundamental processes of nature and its unity and diversity in the contrasting terms 'polarity' (*Polarität*) and 'intensification' (*Steigerung*), each of these keeping nature in perpetual flux and change. This is illustrated by an episode from the late 1780s. Holding a prism against a whitewashed wall to demonstrate how, as Isaac Newton had shown in his *Optics* (1704), light would be split up by refraction into its constituent colours, Goethe found to his surprise that, instead of displaying the expected rainbow spectrum of colours, the wall remained white. He experienced a flash of revelation, which he laboured for the next 20 years to prove in his own *Theory of Colours* (1810). Newton, he believed, and after Newton the Enlightenment approach generally, had been in the profoundest sense wrong in its one-sided passion for analysis and dissection. In splitting up light (or breaking down any other natural phenomenon) the

Enlightenment had, said Goethe, been 'putting Nature on the rack' (quoted in Eliot and Stern, 1979, p.1), violating its essential living, God-given unity and harmony. In a similar spirit of aversion to the dispassionate scientific analysis characteristic of the Enlightenment, viewed as cold, heartless and unfeeling, Wordsworth, in his *Lyrical Ballads* (1798), expressed a thought akin to Goethe's: 'We murder to dissect.'

Similarly, John Keats objected that the rationalism of the scientific method and Enlightenment philosophy suppressed the promptings of the imagination and the intuitions of the poet:

> Philosophy will clip an angel's wings,
> Conquer all mysteries by rule and line,
> Empty the haunted air and gnomèd[13] mine –
> Unweave a rainbow.

> (*Lamia*, 1819, part II, ll.234–7)

Nature, with or without the guiding hand of God, was increasingly seen as an independent force larger than, rather than controllable by, humankind.

To regard the universe, as the Enlightenment had done, as a kind of elaborate machine, whirring away to all eternity in accordance with unalterable physical laws, which struck many at the time as a wonderful confirmation of the rationality of the universe and even a proof of God's existence and benevolence, came to seem oppressive and constricting. It gave nature, so to speak, no chance to breathe. It misunderstood nature and gave a distorted view of it. To the Romantics, nature was not mechanistic but organic, growing, changing, developing. People too, far from being predetermined structures, were living creatures – vital, not just being but *becoming*. Goethe's *Faust* expresses the idea of nature as a stepping stone to a spiritual realm as well as the idea that both people and nature are caught up in a whirl of dynamic, creative change. Science itself became more attuned to the idea of nature as an active force. Humphry Davy's 'dynamical chemistry' suggested that a single, unifying force or principle provided the key to understanding the natural universe and the chemical behaviours of substances. Romanticism focused on the possibility of greater, less predictable or intelligible forces at work behind the surface of things.

This sense of nature's power was also implicit in the aesthetics of the sublime. Cliffs, storms and gigantic waves were conceived of as anarchic forces subject to no influence other than their own power. There was a growing taste for 'wild' nature to be found in previously neglected wildernesses such as the Scottish Highlands, the mountainous areas of the Lakes and the immensity of the Alps (evident in the storm in Canto III of *Childe Harold's Pilgrimage*). This view of a disorderly nature,

---

[13] Inhabited by underground gnomes.

present to a modest extent in various eighteenth-century texts (including Rousseau's works and some of the *Olney Hymns* you have studied; see hymns 2:85 and 3:15 and Block 3, Unit 10), became dominant in the Romantic era. The natural world was not necessarily a definable pattern of perfect, harmonious order, as the 'argument from design' had claimed, but something far more unpredictable and unfathomable. Thus artists such as John Constable and J.M.W. Turner turned from established modes of picturesque composition, in which nature was clearly ordered, framed and tamed, to represent its wilder aspects, from storms to dark clouds and looming mountains. The Romantics cast aside the Enlightenment's more reassuring visions of a scientific mastery of nature.

For Wordsworth and Byron, however, nature's powers were also a source of solace. The divine power that Wordsworth saw at work in the landscape brought him close to the quiet beauties appreciated by Rousseau, who had outlined his religious beliefs in *Émile* (1762). For Wordsworth, who was influenced by the pantheist views of the Dutch philosopher Spinoza (1632–77), God was not merely the creator of nature but immanent in nature. His divine spirit was in the lakes and mountains, inspiring

> a sense sublime
> Of something far more deeply interfused,
> Whose dwelling is the light of setting suns,
> And the round ocean and the living air,
> And the blue sky, and in the mind of man –
> A motion and a spirit that impels
> All thinking things, all objects of all thought,
> And rolls through all things.

(*Tintern Abbey*, 1798, ll.97–104)

Byron was attracted to the views of Rousseau and Wordsworth of nature as a source of purity and simplicity (see Block 6, Units 29–30). Constable visited and painted the beach at Brighton in part because of its reputation as a place offering simple, healthy pleasures (including the sea air which he felt would benefit members of his family suffering ill health) and a refuge from the normal business of life (see Plate 17.24 in the Illustrations Book, *The Sea near Brighton*). The Romantics thus celebrated the quieter beauties of nature as well as its more 'sublime' and terrifying aspects. Those who sought solace in nature nevertheless agreed that its external appearances masked something much deeper and incomprehensible to the human mind, and that the individual was part of nature and partook of the mysterious entity underlying it. Experiencing the natural world came to be seen as a means of testing the powers and limits of one's own understanding and feelings.

To Rousseau, Wordsworth and others, inspired in part by an idealized pastoral vision of rural labour inherited from a longstanding literary tradition, the organic and restorative powers of nature were seen as a retreat from the man-made filth and quest for material wealth that came with advances in technology and industry. Rousseau felt strongly that the mining of the earth for its mineral wealth was a fool's mission:

> he [man] scours the entrails of the earth and descends into its depths, risking his life and health, in search of imaginary gains to replace the true blessings which it offered him spontaneously when he was capable of enjoying them. He flees the sun and the light, which he is no longer worthy of seeing, he buries himself alive, and rightly so, since he no longer deserves to live in the light of day. The quarries, pits, forges, furnaces and a world of anvils, hammers, smoke and flame take the place of the sweet images of rustic labour. Haggard faces of wretches languishing in the foul vapours of the pits, black Vulcans and hideous Cyclops, this is the picture that the mines offer us deep down in the earth, in place of the sight of verdure and flowers, azure sky, loving shepherds and sturdy labourers on its surface.
>
> (Rousseau, 1979, p.113)

Wordsworth likewise protested at industrialization, urbanization and commercialization. In a sonnet of 1807 he wrote:

> The world is too much with us; late and soon,
> Getting and spending, we lay waste our powers:
> Little we see in Nature that is ours;
> We have given our hearts away, a sordid boon!
>
> (Gardner, 1991, p.507)

These conflicting ideas of natural paradise and natural menace continue to play out in our own time, creating ambiguous impulses about whether the natural world is something we should revere or subdue.

EXERCISE   The discussion above confirms the general cultural shift outlined in point 9 of the Course Introduction list ('A growing appreciation of both the dynamism and restorative powers of nature and of its intimate connection with human thought, morality and feelings'). But can you think of any ways in which it over-simplifies the evidence you have considered in this course?

DISCUSSION   You may have thought of ways in which industry continued to harness the powers of nature, for example at New Lanark, or of the ways that the scientific research of Humphry Davy and others continued the Enlightenment quest to demystify and explain the natural world through observation, analysis and experiment. The Enlightenment approach certainly did not disappear with the onset of Romanticism.

Romanticism, the self and the individual

The Romantics developed to the highest degree of intensity Rousseau's quest for self-exploration. Like him, they saw their innermost self as part of nature rather than something separate from it, and placed the discovery of that self at the heart of their concerns. They also saw the individual self or personal identity as something multifaceted and ever-changing. Inspired by John Locke, who had analysed the nature of human consciousness, some Enlightenment thinkers (including Diderot) had already glimpsed the possibility of a complex, unstable personal identity or self. This materialist philosophy made a person's attitudes and behaviour contingent on environmental and educational influences, and hence modifiable. But it was not until the Romantic era that the consequences of this, and the problematic issue of discovering a coherent identity or unified self in the midst of changing or fractured identities, were more fully explored.

Possibly inspired by Rousseau's lakeside reveries, Wordsworth's poems speak of the landscape of the Lakes as intimately bound up with the poet-narrator's own identity, mentality and personal development from child to adult. Byron emulated this idea of self-discovery through travel and landscape in *Childe Harold's Pilgrimage*, in which the inner identity and self-awareness of the poet-narrator seem to merge with those of the poem's hero. You may feel that there is sometimes a degree of posturing, posing and self-indulgence in this obsession with self. The quest for the elusive 'self' perhaps had its origin in the basic attitude at the heart of Rousseau's *Confessions*, an attitude at once profoundly innovatory and disquieting through its elevation of the importance of the individual: namely the notion that I, the writer, am unique among people on this earth. Self-centredness as such was not new. The French Renaissance writer Michel de Montaigne (1533–92) devoted his *Essays* to the exploration of himself, yet he succeeded in making his self-portrait congenial and attractive. Before him the German Renaissance artist Albrecht Dürer (1471–1528) had indulged in self-advertisement through his self-portraits, in one of which he even represented himself as Christ (see Figure C.1). But the tendency really revived and accelerated in the Romantic era, with the simultaneous emergence of writers who took themselves extremely seriously and a public eager to explore with them the depths of individual personality rather than the predictable attributes of Enlightenment 'Man'. Autobiography became an act of self-projection which sometimes featured the attitudinizing already apparent in Rousseau's *Confessions*. On meeting Byron in 1816, Stendhal noted that 'Lord Byron greatly resembled Rousseau in the sense that he was constantly occupied with himself and with the effect he produced on others' (quoted in Anderson, 1985, p.369). The same may be said of Napoleon, ever conscious of his own persona, who did not tolerate rivals or opposition but in his boundless self-assertion demanded – and almost always received – uncritical devotion and obedience. Mme de Staël claimed that throughout his rule Napoleon 'sought to set up his gigantic *Me* in the place of humankind' (see Anthology I, p.120).

Staël's impression of such colossal egotism, such Luciferian pride, is a long way from the sociability of the *philosophes*, the amiable clubability of Hume. Humphry Davy, possibly inspired by the language and example of Wordsworth, even applied an autobiographical approach in a scientific treatise, his book on nitrous oxide: *Researches Chemical and Philosophical, Chiefly Concerning Nitrous Oxide and its Respiration* (1800). In his *Discourse Introductory to a Course of Lectures on Chemistry* (1802), Davy perceived the mainspring of human interest in the investigation of nature as a wish to allay 'the restlessness of his [man's] desires' (Anthology II, p.152). The sentiment is distinctly Faustian. The brilliantly versatile and imaginative architect Sir John Soane, who idolized both Rousseau and Napoleon, sometimes showed himself to be

Figure C.1   Albrecht Dürer, Self-Portrait, *1500, oil on lime panel, 67 x 49 cm, Alte Pinakothek, Munich.*

a monster of self-absorbed egotism and insatiable ambition. Goethe's Faust is a man of no fixed identity in the sense of a stable identifiable inner self: his susceptibility to external influence is a source of self-torture as he struggles to acquire some kind of personal authenticity. His only consistent characteristic is, perhaps, his endless need to change and develop: there can be no stability in the way in which he perceives himself or others perceive him. Similarly, Unit 31 on the Royal Pavilion suggests that the Prince Regent was attempting to express through architectural styles the eccentricities of his own identity. Delacroix also tried to invest his innermost being in his art. His voyage to Morocco in 1832 formed part of his attempt to define his individual identity as an artist. And yet, paradoxically, he struggled to convince others that he was no reckless Romantic but an artist still dedicated to classical purity, discipline and balance. In this case, the attempt to establish an identity brought personal complexities into conflict with a well-established (and desirable) aesthetic category. Whereas Rousseau seemed reasonably confident in proclaiming goodness as a constant characteristic central to his identity, later Romantics were less confident about the identifiability of the self and their ability to discover its true essence. Their personal quest was often a stimulus to melancholic disappointment.

The Enlightenment had celebrated the independent-minded individual, the 'great man' such as Isaac Newton, while assuming that all like-minded, rational individuals would reach a consensus on large issues. This confidence in an ultimate consensus was challenged in some quarters. As Evangelicalism developed in eighteenth-century Britain, for example, the emphasis on the personal and on individual salvation was in some sense perceived as a threat to the cohesion of society. 'Begging your Honour's pardon,' says Humphrey Clinker to his master in Tobias Smollett's novel of that name (1771), 'May not the new light of God's grace shine upon the poor and the ignorant in their humility, as well as upon the wealthy and the philosopher in all his pride of human learning?' (Smollett, 1967, p.170). For the Enlightenment _philosophe_ the egalitarian thrust of the question was a troublesome impertinence. Gibbon stressed 'the immense distance between the man of learning and the _illiterate_ peasant' (Gibbon, 1998, p.190; original emphasis), implying the continuing necessity of a traditional social and political hierarchy holding the ring against nonconformist (in every sense) outsiders.

In the Romantic era the uniqueness of the individual moved centre-stage, and the possibility of shared values seemed either less exciting or less relevant. While Mozart's Don Giovanni as a character would have caused ripples of concern to an enlightened mind set on discovering universal social and moral guidelines, he was an object of fascination to the Romantics, who celebrated the outsider and the rebel and prioritized individual liberty – and, as you may recall, suppressed as inadequate and bathetic the final chorus celebrating a return to normality after the just deserts suffered by Don Giovanni. (This part of the opera is still seldom performed.) Like the Marquis de Sade, Don Giovanni represents the individual at odds with the needs and conventions of society at large, and the potential dangers – and thrills – of rampant egotism. Napoleon, like Rousseau and the mythical Don Giovanni, was a unique individual admired for the colour, energy and daring of his personality. A courageous free spirit, his rise and fall were seen by many Romantics across Europe after 1815 as a dazzling burst of sunlight against the backdrop of dreary, reactionary, morally bankrupt regimes. Goethe's character Faust embarks on his journey of self-discovery as an individual who has been failed by systems of knowledge promising universal, consensual solutions. In Britain the Prince Regent demonstrated a strongly individualistic imagination in his collection of exotic plans for the Brighton Pavilion, while Soane's Museum in London was the storehouse of the extraordinary interests of a unique mind. Like the Pavilion, the museum functioned, on one level, as a self-image of its creator. Delacroix's *Sardanapalus* is another representation of destructive and glamorous individualism. To the Romantics, then, there was something heroic about the unique, defiant individual, a judgement which has inspired many cultural developments closer to our own time.

EXERCISE The discussion in this section has supported the claims made in point 3 of the cultural shifts listed in the Course Introduction ('An increasing emphasis on the self, introspection, identity and individualism'). But did everything in the period you have studied fragment so openly and decisively into unbridled individualism?

DISCUSSION Think again of Owen's New Lanark, of Mrs Marcet's attempts to share her knowledge of chemistry with others, or of the warnings implicit in Goethe's *Faust* of the dangers associated with personal ambition. Through such qualifying examples we can see how the values of Romanticism were contested by alternative objectives. Cultural change is a complex process involving competing forces.

Romanticism was often characterized by paradox. On the one hand, the growth of national consciousness and the concern with the individual self suggested infinitely variable ways of seeing the world, a view of truth as multifaceted and pluralist. On the other hand, many Romantics sought to apprehend a kind of unity underlying the ephemeral and the particular. As you will see below, they sought access to a kind of truth that transcended the shifting illusions of the specific and the individual.

The heroic, the exotic and the lure of travel

The Romantic cult of the unique individual helped to crystallize a concept of heroism that remains central to western culture. Romantic heroes were nearly always male, even when the author was female, as with the hero of Mary Shelley's *Frankenstein* (1808). Mme de Staël's projection in her novels (notably *Corinne*, 1807) of herself as man's equal, combining an enlightened mind with a sensibility and willpower, is an interesting exception. Jane Austen's heroines, however sprightly and talented, invariably find satisfaction in marriage to dominant men with an active role in a masculine world: Mr Darcy, Mr Knightley, Captain Wentworth, for instance.

Napoleon was the unrivalled archetype of what Stendhal called 'the modern hero', the individual potential pushed to limits of power and achievement unparalleled and undreamed-of since the days of Alexander the Great and Julius Caesar. Portrayed by artists such as David and Antoine-Jean Gros as a dynamic and charismatic man of destiny, he also suffered a tragic downfall that provided the blueprint for the Romantic obsession with heroic striving, disappointment and loss. Looking back, Napoleon himself exclaimed, 'What a novel my life has been!' (*Quel roman que ma vie!*) – virtually the equivalent of 'What a romantic life!' The Romantics took the classical myth of Prometheus and turned it into a modern parable. Prometheus, a demi-god, brought to humankind the divine gift of fire and civilization, and for this he was punished by being tied to a rock and subjected to eternal torment. Napoleon's fate at St Helena made the comparison with Prometheus almost commonplace. Schubert set to music Goethe's poem *Prometheus* (1773), with both words and music celebrating the hero rebel's defiance of fate. Goethe's *Faust* also expresses perfectly the type of the fallible hero, striving against the odds to discover salvation in new and beneficial forms of knowledge, in the face of the growing inadequacy of the Christian and Enlightenment certainties of the old world. Byron and Stendhal were deeply influenced by the Napoleonic phenomenon; indeed Byron seemed, in his colourful life, to wish to emulate the energy, charisma and inventiveness of his spiritual mentor. Napoleon was more than a military hero: he represented a mentality of heroic celebrity and transformative power. And in both Napoleon and his admirers there was often a tragic discrepancy between aspiration and outcome. Byron's poetic 'hero', Childe Harold, somehow fails to achieve any real objective in his heroic quest, and there seem to be echoes in the poem of the sense of loss emanating from the failed dreams of the semi-divine Napoleon. It has in fact been suggested that this sense of loss, gathering in intensity during the post-Napoleonic era, was the wellspring of what we most commonly understand as Romanticism (see Mowat, 1937, p.77, and Brookner, 2000, p.3).

The human aspiration towards quasi-divine power drew together the worlds of politics and religion in many ways. The Evangelical collection of *Olney Hymns* included references to the bloody, heroic self-sacrifice of Christ, and many history paintings of the late eighteenth and early nineteenth centuries borrowed religious iconography (for example, traditional poses of the dead or dying Christ) in their depictions of revolutionary and military heroes and martyrs. David's *The Death of Marat* (Figure C.2; see also Plate 9.7 in the Illustrations Book) uses a pose derived from the iconography of the *pietà*, the traditional representation of the dead Christ cradled in the arms of the mourning Virgin Mary. Long after the disillusionment and the dissolution of Napoleon's empire, there lingered a sense of mourning and a continuing yearning for the heroic.

If notions of modern heroism answered a need for excitement, this function was also fulfilled by a growing interest in travel and the 'foreign'. In the late eighteenth and early nineteenth centuries, the conventional Enlightenment Grand Tour, taking in the sites of ancient Rome, also began to accommodate a greater interest in the contemporary. Locations such as the Grand Duchy of Weimar (where Goethe flourished) or Mme de Staël's seat at Coppet in Switzerland

Figure C.2 Jacques-Louis David, The Death of Marat, *1793, oil on canvas, 160.7 x 124.8 cm, Musées royaux des Beaux-Arts de Belgique, Brussels. Photo: Cussac.*

became staging posts for European travellers and intellectuals from as far afield as Britain and Russia. They were keen to inhabit the same spaces as their cultural and intellectual 'heroes'. (Think of Byron's visits to the field of Waterloo and to sites associated with Rousseau, as portrayed in *Childe Harold's Pilgrimage*.) Celebrity, novelty and unfamiliarity were equally attractive to those selecting destinations. In the 1770s Archdeacon William Coxe took his aristocratic charges in a novel direction on the 'Northern Tour' of Scandinavia, Poland and Russia. Mary Wollstonecraft toured Sweden.

The quest for the unique and the colourful also manifested itself in a growing taste for the 'exotic'. The word was used favourably in relation to the strange, the remote and the unfamiliar. Wordsworth even used it (perhaps ironically) in relation to the white Palladian villas springing up across the Lake District, for they contrasted in his mind so wildly with the cottages in local stone that seemed to grow organically from the land. Paintings and writings on the subject of exotic lands had played an important part in Enlightenment culture, usually with a view to reinforcing Enlightenment values. French writers, for example, had often referred to the customs and societies of locations such as Persia in their attempts to make indirect criticisms of their own country that would successfully elude the censor. They had also represented the newly 'discovered' Pacific islands as a utopia of freedom and happiness. Painters too depicted far-distant lands in order to meet a demand for exotic and Oriental decorative schemes and subjects (see Figure C.3). At the same time, there was among the wealthy great enthusiasm for Chinese-inspired designs of decoration, artefacts and furniture (chinoiseries), as well as respect for the achievements of Chinese civilization generally.

The Romantics took over this eclectic interest in the exotic and appropriated it for their own purposes. Knowledge and experience of foreign lands and identification with them (or, more usually, with stereotypical impressions of them) became another way of testing one's own identity and highlighting the infinite variations of the human psyche. Byron donned exotic costumes, including outfits meant to symbolize the rebel and brigand Greeks, in the cause of whose national independence from the Turks he died in 1824. The exotic formed another aspect of the general striving for difference, individuality, the mysterious and something beyond the old social and moral certainties. Gros, inspired by Napoleon's Egyptian campaign, suggested both the passivity and the ferocity of Oriental figures in his depictions of episodes from that part of Napoleon's career. At the Royal Pavilion designs approved by the Prince Regent expressed through Mogul architecture ideas of power and empire which he saw as part of his self-projection. Such designs also reflected escapist fantasies of the type appropriate to Romantic adventurers wishing to range beyond the confines of western culture. This use of the exotic as a form of escapism, a site of sensuous desire and fantasy for the Romantic disillusioned with western

Figure C.3   Nicolas-Pierre Pitou the Younger, after Charles-Amédée-Phillipe Vanloo, The Sultana's Lunch, *1783, porcelain plaque, 40.5 x 48.5 cm, Musée National de Céramique, Sèvres. Photo: © RMN/M. Beck-Coppola.*

During the Enlightenment period, the Oriental and exotic were enfolded in a culture of civilized gentility. The painting from which this plaque is derived, Vanloo's The Sultana Being Served by Black and White Eunuchs, *was exhibited at the Paris Salon of 1775 and was commissioned by Louis XV's mistress, Madame du Barry, who wished it to serve as a tapestry design.*

convention, came to the fore in Delacroix's 1827–8 painting of a suicidal eastern despot's order for mass murder, *The Death of Sardanapalus*.

Travel and the Grand Tour had been important during the Enlightenment period as a means of self-improvement, education and broadening of knowledge and experience. There were occasional women travellers, at least women of means, excluded from other more conventional forms of education in 'non-feminine' subjects such as science and politics (see Dolan, 2001, p.5). Elizabeth Montagu (1720–1800), for instance, was fortunate in that she received a better education than most women. Famous as 'Queen of the Bluestockings', her intellect and wit were legendary. She went on to be an important philanthropist and writer and, after the death of her husband in 1774, she commissioned the building of

Montagu House in Portman Square, London. Hungry for new experiences, she travelled to France in 1763 and was one of many British women fascinated by the differences between that country and their own. She was intrigued by French churches and particularly by nunneries, which seemed to many Englishwomen a shocking form of incarceration. For such women, travel, with its accompanying traditions of sketching, keeping a journal and letter-writing, provided a kind of training in social, historical and political observation. Escaping the confines of the domestic in order to walk or travel was one of the few ways in which many women could express freedom of spirit, as you may recall from the fictional example of Elizabeth Bennet, the heroine of Jane Austen's novel *Pride and Prejudice* (1813), who loves to roam the fields as an escape from house-bound domesticity and the follies of her mother, and who relishes the chance of a tour of the Peak District. For real women of greater means, travel to the Continent opened wider horizons. Banished from France by Napoleon because her books were implicitly critical of his regime, Mme de Staël travelled widely in Europe, notably in Italy and Germany. Then, escaping Napoleon's power altogether, she pitted her own person and intellect unreservedly against what she felt to be the despotism, political and cultural, which he came to represent. In Vienna, St Petersburg, Stockholm and London, where she was lionized, she played a political role more usually confined to men, liaising between the leaders of the allied coalition against Napoleon.

For men there were other advantages to be gained from travel abroad. It was a qualification for entry into the diplomatic service, or universities, or institutions of painting, sculpture and architecture, or societies for the advancement of learning. Humphry Davy travelled extensively in connection with his researches into agriculture. He also regularly explored the outdoors for leisure purposes such as angling, shooting, fishing and amateur geology. Sponsored by one particular learned society, the African Association, the explorer Mungo Park opened up the geography and culture of parts of Africa previously unknown to Europeans. Closer to home, as the revolutionary and Napoleonic wars closed much of continental Europe to the Grand Tour, it became fashionable for British tourists to visit wilder parts of Britain itself, notably the Lakes, as a means of improving their aesthetic taste. 'Picturesque' tourists looked at the landscape through the eyes of painters and aspired to produce their own commemorative sketches by applying methods of composition outlined by William Gilpin. Soane inherited an Enlightenment enthusiasm for educational travel and commissioned from Joseph Gandy watercolour paintings of landscapes and buildings. In other respects, however, his interest in 'other' cultures was distinctly Romantic and sometimes bordered on morbidity.

The Romantics inherited the eighteenth-century penchant for travel, but often changed the emphasis from knowledge and understanding of the world and 'mankind' to travel as self-discovery. Following Rousseau's example, Wordsworth established the type of the Romantic wanderer who encounters the landscape in order to test and extend his own sense of identity. So did Schubert in his contemplative setting of Goethe's *Wanderer's Night Song*. Similarly, in *Childe Harold's Pilgrimage* Byron seemed to subvert the tradition of educational travel: his hero wanders apparently aimlessly across Europe. Like Wordsworth, his restless 'hero' became a part of the natural scenes around him – so much so that self-discovery became an objective fraught with difficulties, the poet's self being elusively embodied in an ever-changing landscape.

EXERCISE   This section has highlighted the Romantics' attachment to notions of the heroic and the exotic, and has stressed changing attitudes to travel and outdoor walking or 'wandering'. Pause for a moment to reflect on any potential risks and benefits of this process of isolating, identifying and making generalizations about Romanticism or cultural trends.

DISCUSSION   Summarizing and isolating the main characteristics of Romanticism or cultural trends may carry risks of over-simplification, but these processes also allow us to view more clearly and critically the larger picture. (They may even help us to view in a new light more recent trends in our own society, such as the cults of celebrity, travel and self-discovery.)

Romanticism, the unknowable and the inexplicable

The greatest difference between the Enlightenment and Romanticism was the latter's undermining of the idea that there are clear, objectively true answers to any of the questions we might ask. The human mind came to be seen as something subjective rather than something that could, with sufficient intelligence and perseverance, tap into a world of universally valid truths. It is one of the ironies of intellectual history that one of the thinkers ultimately responsible for this great shift was the German philosopher Immanuel Kant (1724–1804), a man who was in every important way committed to the beliefs and ideals of the Enlightenment.[14] Kant argued that human experience has the form it has because the human mind and perceptual apparatus have a special structure which they impose on whatever we encounter. For example, just as the world looks red to you if you put on spectacles with red lenses, so (in Kant's view) we experience things as existing in space and time because our senses have space and time built into their structure, and so on for a dozen other very general features of human experience. How things are in themselves, Kant stated, we can never know: all we

---

[14] We are grateful to our colleague Dr Robert Wilkinson for this section on Kant and Fichte.

can know is how they appear to beings which have the mental-perceptual structure that we have. This doctrine seemed to Kant's successors, notably the philosopher Johann Gottlieb Fichte (1762–1814), whom you met briefly in the context of German aesthetics, to be inconsistent. Fichte denied that there are 'things in themselves', and what he was left with, accordingly, was a view in which reality is only mental in nature. For Fichte, reality consisted not of a subject experiencing an objective world, but only of a subject (a mind) which in a certain sense *creates* its world. It was Fichte's extensively modified version of Kantianism which was the most important influence on the Romantic view of the mind in general and the imagination in particular as truly creative; and it is this Romantic doctrine which lies behind many ideas that are with us still. It is the ultimate source, for instance, of fashionable views which assert that truths in politics, morality, culture, psychology and the like are in some sense 'relative' or 'subjective'. This view is not, however, all-pervasive. In our times science, scholarship and other forms of appeal to experience perpetuate the quest for objective truth and common standards championed by the Enlightenment.

If you put Fichte's view together with other Romantic perceptions of the self and the mind attuned to larger quasi-divine forces lying beneath and beyond the world of physical appearances, you can appreciate how the potential for inadequacy, despair and disillusionment often accompanied much of the elation or exultation experienced in striving to grasp ultimate reality. To the Romantics, truth or reality was not to be found in the sphere of the human and the physical, which had stimulated Enlightenment minds, but in something far less tangible or accessible. As Romanticism developed, so more intense and pathological forms of melancholy and world-weariness (variously known as *ennui*, *Weltschmerz* or spleen) became more prevalent. Those who persisted in heroic striving knew they were deploying limited human faculties in order to try to grasp the infinite, the unknowable and the unnameable. This is one of the dilemmas at the heart of Goethe's *Faust*. There is no simple interpretation of the play, however, as Goethe continued to balance potential despair against the rationality of classicism, an enlightening and controlling force to which (like Delacroix) he continued to express allegiance.

Edmund Burke's notion of the sublime was well suited to this new emphasis on the unknowable and the infinite, and it became central to the Romantic mindset. Turner's paintings and Byron's poetry both describe scenes in which human figures and characters are subjected to overpowering forces that defy rational understanding. In *Childe Harold's Pilgrimage*, Byron wrote:

> I live not in myself, but I become
> Portion of that around me; and to me
> High mountains are a feeling

(Canto III, stanza 72)

– a sentiment that would have been incomprehensible to Dr Johnson. For the Romantics, the sublime invoked feelings of inadequacy and melancholy that came from a self-conscious focus on the limits of human intelligence.

One of the consequences of the Romantics' despair at the unattainability of certain knowledge and fixed truths was a celebration of art forms that fell short of completeness of expression. Music and poetry were valued for their evocative powers, suggesting without ever aspiring to fix meaning, whereas sculpture, as an art form exploiting the physical, material and three-dimensional, was frequently regarded as inherently explicit, rather than evocative, in its references. Composed of tangible, physical matter, it imitated closely the forms and substance of real life. As the medium was inherently specific and earth-bound, Romantic sculptors worked hard on expression, pose and composition in order to suggest more open and evocative meanings (see Figure C.4). Music was the most obviously Romantic of all art forms, being intangible and inherently indefinable. Attempts to analyse and dissect its meaning were seen as missing the point. (This did not deter some commentators from ventures at definition; E.T.A. Hoffmann (1776–1822), for instance, sought to describe Beethoven's Romantic qualities in an article of 1813.) While some music was programmatic, intended to 'copy' nature or tell a story (Schubert's songs are a prime example of this), its essential appeal was perceived to be subliminal – speaking to the emotions, not to reason. Schubert's orchestral and instrumental music does not seem to be 'about' anything in the way that his settings of 'Der Erl-König', 'Prometheus' or 'Ganymed' are musical representations of Goethe's poems. Non-representational music evokes moods and states of feeling rather than making rational statements. But even a more or less rational plot and story-line could prompt more questions than answers. For the Romantics, Mozart's Don Giovanni became the ultimate enigmatic, ambiguous figure around whom no universal, human moral judgements could coalesce; it was necessary for an unintelligible hell to deal with him.

Thus the incomplete work, the sketch, the unfathomable myth and the fragment came into vogue. You have heard how in some of his songs (for example, 'Gretchen at the Spinning-Wheel'; see Block 6, Unit 28) Schubert cultivated 'unfinished' endings. Soane, meanwhile, encouraged students to set down their first bold, spontaneous inspirations: 'Nothing can be more useful to the student than his own theoretical dreams of magnificent compositions produced by a warm imagination' (Sixth Royal Academy Lecture; Soane, 2000, p.151). Similarly, the Royal Pavilion at Brighton expressed the qualities of the fragmentary and of the unknowable in its fantasy architecture, resonating with Thomas Moore's poem *Lalla Rookh* (1817) in its celebration of the mysterious and fantastic. Delacroix composed his paintings in ways that seemed illogical to those versed in the rules of perspective and, along with Constable and Turner, cultivated an unfinished sketchiness in his brushwork that always seemed to leave open the possibility of further amendment. Indeed, it

Figure C.4   Anton Dietrich, Bust of Beethoven *(detail),
1821, Museen der Stadt Wien, Vienna. Photo: © Museen
der Stadt Wien, Vienna.*

*An inscription on the pedestal states that this bust was
modelled from life in 1821. 'I will take Fate by the
throat,' Beethoven declared, triumphantly outfacing
deafness and adversity (quoted in Sullivan, 1964, p.38).*

was common practice for artists to retouch their works right up to the
moment of the opening of an exhibition. Delacroix suggested that
conventional distinctions between reason and an irrational soul were
misleading. In his view, such false intellectual distinctions or categories
violated and insulted the impenetrability of nature and failed to do
justice to the complexity of artistic and aesthetic experience. It was only
by abandoning conventional ways of looking at our responses to art and

experience that an artist could even contemplate an attempt to 'penetrate the veil' separating more common minds from an ultimate reality.

Romanticism, art and the artist

Romantic ideas on art had a significance that extended far beyond the aesthetic. As you have seen, Napoleon was the most illustrious of many who both patterned their lives on examples from history and drama, and further wove the fictions of art into their lives to embroider and inspire a compelling variety of legends. The model of a creative mind and imagination theorized by Fichte transformed the way in which art and artists were seen, and helped to formulate a notion of the artistic genius that has coloured our view of artists ever since. In contrast to the Enlightenment idea of the imagination as recipient and reprocessor of sense impressions and experience, the Romantic imagination liberated itself and assumed its own individual capacity for original creativity. The artist, as the painter Benjamin Haydon (1786–1846) insisted, was 'sent into the world not to obey laws but to give them' (quoted in Anderson, 1985, p.332). In contrast to the well-balanced and learned practitioner (the skilled artificer and purveyor of finely crafted artefacts for aristocratic patrons, as often conceived of during the Enlightenment), the poet, artist or composer, in the eyes of the Romantics, was a man[15] apart, an independent spirit, a law unto himself, possessed of prophetic qualities and a vital inspiration without which, in the words of Percy Bysshe Shelley (1792–1822), 'a man cannot say, "I will compose poetry"' (Halsted, 1969, p.94). In the eighteenth century it was held that a man could certainly write poetry if he but set his mind to it by learning and applying the accepted rules of versification. Both Voltaire and Dr Johnson were as much admired for their neoclassical verse as for their prose works. By contrast Shelley, in *A Defence of Poetry* (1821), expounded the exalted conception of poetry as 'something divine', 'the centre and circumference of knowledge', something which, like light for Goethe, transcended Enlightenment observation and analysis 'to bring light and fire from those eternal regions where the owl-winged faculty of calculation dare not ever soar' (Halsted, 1969, pp.94–5). Again, clearly, we have here an allusion to Prometheus – a comparison between him and the semi-divine poet, with his unique 'gift', his ability to perceive beyond the sphere of reason and the ken of ordinary mortals, and to communicate to them his special vision. With the eye of imagination, the poet or artist believed he could penetrate the surface, the outward appearance of reality, reaching through to an ultimate reality. Blake distinguished the corporeal or physical eye from the eye of the imagination, which looks *through* rather than just *at* creation.

Self-expression by the artist came to acquire a greater importance than following 'the rules', which were in any case often regarded as outdated

---

[15] The Romantic genius was generally gendered as male.

and artificial. We can already perceive something of this emancipation in works preceding Romantic theory. The order and structure of Mozart's music, for example, continued to satisfy the classical requirement for reason, balance and discipline, while using such a framework in uniquely original expressive ways. By the nineteenth century the untrammelled 'genius' of Mozart was contrasted with the mediocrity of his hard-working but uninspired contemporary at the Viennese court, Antonio Salieri. Indeed, in his miniature drama *Mozart and Salieri*, Alexander Pushkin (1799–1837) based his plot on a rumour that Salieri murdered Mozart out of envy for his genius.[16] Similarly, Constable and Turner began to paint nature in new ways, uninhibited by preceding formulae. And yet it took time for many of their critics to accept fully this growing emphasis on a personalized, individual style based on the artist's claim to a unique and overriding inner vision. 'A painter', in the words of Caspar David Friedrich, 'must not paint merely what he sees before him, but also what he sees within himself' (quoted in Thorlby, 1966, p.151). The imagination as conceived by the Romantics could not be subject to any laws, but constituted (in the minds of Romantic theorists) a more hopeful means of attaining absolute truth. This truth was, as you have seen in your study of German aesthetics, of a kind far more elusive, spiritual and indefinable than the scientific truths about the physical world to which the Enlightenment aspired. In Germany thinkers such as Wackenroder wrote of art as a form of personal salvation in a way that owed much to developments in religious thought. Goethe's Faust can be seen as an embodiment of the Romantic artist, ceaselessly restless and creative but set loose in a world of destructive forces.[17] For Delacroix, the artist had to cast aside conventional standards and preoccupations, and (in accordance with Rousseau) escape the platitudes of normal social intercourse, in order to unleash creativity. Once released, this creativity would enable the artist to communicate through art with other free spirits.

We have come a long way from the spirit of the Enlightenment, with its wit, irony, good sense, good humour and moderation. After Mozart and Hume in Block 1, and with the exception of some parts of *Faust*, there is little pure humour in the texts you have studied, though you may have spotted in some of them examples of a bitter, sardonic irony.[18] Our course might have included other well-known humorous texts from the period – you have already had a taste, for instance, of some of the many satirical drawings created, such as those by Thomas Rowlandson and James Gillray. But humour was not often comfortable for a Romantic

[16] This is a theme in the modern play by Peter Schaffer, *Amadeus* (1979), well known in its film version (1984).

[17] Thomas Mann explored this potentiality in the Faust figure in *Doktor Faustus* (1947).

[18] In Audio 5, *Romanticism in Practice*, Robert Wilkinson refers to the concept of 'Romantic irony'.

sensibility, as it demanded a certain critical detachment from the world and oneself as well as a modicum of sociability and good spirits. The Romantic was not often of the Salon, society culture that fostered wit and the social graces. Rousseau, notoriously, felt ill at ease in such company and rebelled against its artificiality. Byron, who was born into polite society and revelled in being lionized by it, affected to despise it once he had outraged and fled it. The Romantic was in the wilds, literally and figuratively, communing with nature and with himself. The title of Rousseau's *Reveries of the Solitary Walker* is highly significant. Many of the poems which Schubert set to music are concerned with alienation, loneliness, restlessness and yearning. The Romantics tended to take themselves extremely seriously, obsessed with exploring their own feelings, their inner selves and their sense of personal mission. This could often lead to an overwrought intensity, an attitude merging into the stereotype or parody of the Romantic 'Byronic' attitude fashionable in Europe by the 1820s (see Figure C.5), from *Childe Harold's Pilgrimage* to Pushkin's *Eugene Onegin*. Chateaubriand recalled with some irony:

> In 1822 the man of fashion had to present at first sight the appearance of an unhappy and unhealthy man: he must have something negligent about his person, long nails, the chin partly unshaven, as if the hair had grown ... through forgetfulness in his absent-minded desperation; his hair tousled by the wind, his looks at once deep, sublime, distracted and fateful; his lips contracted in scorn of the human race; his heart weary, 'Byronian', drowned in the dissatisfaction and mystery of life.

(Quoted in Mowat, 1937, p.113)

Chateaubriand's pastiche of the artist as a morbid, pathological personality became a stereotype (discussed with reference to Byron in Video 6, band 1) that has continued to inform images of the artist in our post-Romantic age.

Such views of themselves by Romantic poets and artists might suggest massive egotism on their part. Chateaubriand's description, though exaggerated, is not so far removed from other representations, including Girodet's portrait of Chateaubriand himself (see Figure C.6). But then Kant's theories had facilitated the view of the artist, elaborated by Fichte and exemplified in Shelley, as a demi-god literally able to create his own world. Freed from the obligation to represent an observed reality, Romantic artists felt they could explore the realms of fancy in their search for a more authentic truth than that revealed by the world of external appearances. Goya's grotesque commentaries on contemporary life were based on first-hand observation, but increasingly any pretence at realism gave way to nightmare fantasies and monstrous imaginings (see Figure C.7).

Although artists, writers and composers were freed from the constraints of classicism, many (like Delacroix) chose to retain some of its rational

Figure C.5 Anonymous, The Romantic*, 1825, lithograph, Paris, Bibliothèque Nationale de France.*

discipline. Nevertheless, Gros, Géricault, Delacroix and others set in motion a process of challenging conventional methods of composing history paintings that led to escalating degrees of daring in the work of later Romantics: colours became brighter; action became more violent and off-centre. Gothic disorder, horror and exotic excess, in both subject matter and style, became a means of expressing a newly liberated imagination freed from the bounds of the classical and the familiar. August Wilhelm Schlegel distinguished the modern, progressive spirit of Romanticism from the conservatively classical. His translations into German of Shakespeare's plays, now classics in themselves, bore testimony to his desire to break free from the constraints of classicism. As Romanticism evolved, there was a general feeling that breaking rules of all kinds was almost an obligation. For instance, Soane experimented in innovative ways with classical rules of architecture, although his search for professional respectability also led him to some regrets on this subject.

The Romantics conceived of genius as a unique individual innately endowed with a deep capacity for originality. The Romantic genius was a being of special powers, who worked creatively and spontaneously with instinct, feeling and imagination and was more liberated from rules and restrictions than his Enlightenment counterpart. While Voltaire's praise of Shakespeare was tempered by disapproval of his violations of 'the rules',

Figure C.6   Anne-Louis Girodet-Trioson, François-René, Vicomte de Chateaubriand, Meditating on the Ruins of Rome before a View of the Colosseum, *1811, oil on canvas, 130 x 96 cm, Châteaux de Versailles et de Trianon, France. Photo: © RMN/Gérard Blot.*

by 1818 Stendhal (possibly taking a lead from the earlier German *Sturm und Drang* movement and Goethe) had thrown down the gauntlet to the classicists by proclaiming, 'I am a furious Romantic, that is to say I am for Shakespeare against Racine, for Lord Byron against Boileau' (quoted in Hemmings, 1987, p.165). Even during the Enlightenment, Diderot as art critic had written approvingly of the 'fire' of enthusiasm that artists invested in their preliminary sketches and models, only for it very often to disappear in the too polished finished product. The Romantics aimed to retain this 'fire' in their works and saw 'finish' of all kinds (including the smooth paint finish demanded of high art by the academies) as an anathema. Goya spoke out against the stifling effect of rules on art. The

Figure C.7   Francisco de Goya, The Sleep of Reason
Produces Monsters, *c.1798, etching, Musée des Beaux-
Arts, Lille. Photo: © RMN/Quecq d'Henripret.*

scientific demonstrations arranged by Davy literally threw sparks at his
audiences, as the whizzes and bangs of his experiments aligned him with
the creative fire of the Romantic artist (see Figure C.8). Fired by the
psychic forces of the gods, the Romantic genius transgressed all
traditional boundaries and sometimes became 'possessed'. The cost of
this kind of volatility was for many, as we have seen, a marked exposure
to despair and certainly an interest in nocturnal themes and the darker
aspects of the psyche. The type of the anguished genius close to
madness became well established, exemplified in the poet Cowper and
the architect Soane. Even Stendhal, for all his hero-worship, imputed
madness to Napoleon.

Figure C.8   Joseph Wright of Derby, The Alchymist, in
Search of the Philosopher's Stone, Discovers
Phosphorous, and Prays for the Successful Conclusion
of his Operation, as was the Custom of the Ancient
Chymical Astrologers, *1771, oil on canvas, 127 x
101.6 cm, Derby Museum and Art Gallery. Photo:
Bridgeman Art Library.*

*Prefiguring Romanticism, Wright's dramatic use of light
and shade link 'science' with the irrational sublime, the
supernatural and notions of the creative genius.*

The Enlightenment had instigated a critique of the conventional
boundaries and categories of art. Diderot, for example, promoted the
virtues of genres of painting, such as landscape and still life, that had
always been regarded as 'low' in the hierarchies of the academies, and
he approved a new kind of serious, moral comedy for the expression in
the theatre of moral sentiments. This kind of hybridization of genres
continued throughout the eighteenth century. Mozart's *Don Giovanni*, for

instance, mingles the character types and conventions of serious and comic opera. The Romantics carried this blurring of boundaries much further. There are indications of this mentality in Humphry Davy's determination to sweep away the divisions between areas of scientific investigation in order to discover the underlying unity of nature. Goethe's *Faust*, Schubert's songs and Byron's *Childe Harold's Pilgrimage* are equally adventurous in their invention of new, hybrid genres of artistic expression. What was required were new forms of expression for a modern age. The Romantics pushed to even greater extremes the Enlightenment's rebelliousness and quest for modernity. As industrialization and revolution had brought a new social order, so the need was felt for new kinds of art. In restoration France and across post-Napoleonic Europe generally, including Britain, many Romantics felt themselves increasingly alien to a reactionary political environment, and the call to innovate grew louder.

3   Some final thoughts

As we suggested earlier, the outlines of Enlightenment and Romanticism offered both here and in the Course Introduction are artificial constructions written with benefit of hindsight and in order to try to make sense of a complex phenomenon. Romanticism is harder to define than Enlightenment because of its greater variety and complexity. Not all Romantics thought in the same way or believed in the same things. In politics, for example, there were Romantics who were 'progressive', liberal or left-wing, like Byron or Stendhal, and Romantics who were conservative or even reactionary, such as Chateaubriand, who lent his support to the Bourbon restoration, and Joseph De Maistre, a Catholic who denounced both the French Revolution and the belief in liberty that inspired it. There were nationalists too, like Fichte and Arndt. National self-awareness itself could be multifaceted. It could be associated with a liberal outlook and be denounced as dangerously revolutionary (as it was by Metternich, chancellor of the multinational Austrian empire). Alternatively it might be taken over as part of a conservative philosophy, as with Scott and the later Wordsworth. Goethe, on the other hand, retained his characteristic cosmopolitan balance; while encouraging and contributing to a distinctive German culture, he saw this as part of a European and world culture.

For all the diversity and complexity of 'the Romantic movement' (to use an alternative term for Romanticism), writers, artists, musicians and thinkers in the early nineteenth century were clear about one thing: something fundamental separated their outlook from that of their parents' (and certainly their grandparents') generation. (This conviction is pungently expressed in the quotation from Stendhal that begins the Course Introduction.) That *something* has retained its hold on the imagination and has remained a major, sometimes perhaps *the* major, force in European life; and that *something*, elusive and indefinable as it may often seem in its origins, evolution and characteristics, is what we have invited you to explore through the texts of this course.

EXERCISE   Read the following lines from Byron's dramatic poem *Manfred* (1817) (Act 2, Scene 2, lines 51–6). Compare them with the article 'Philosophe' printed at the end of the Course Introduction. In a couple of sentences, state how the narrator in Byron's lines contrasts with the image of an enlightened *philosophe*.

> My spirit walked not with the souls of men,
> Nor looked upon the earth with human eyes;
> The thirst of their ambition was not mine,
> The aim of their existence was not mine;
> My joys – my griefs – my passions – and my powers,
> Made me a stranger.

DISCUSSION   The sociable, outward-looking and rational *philosophe* has been replaced by an inward-looking, melancholic, other-worldly, emotional and alienated Romantic figure. You may feel that the contrast vividly illustrates the scale of change that occurred in the period you have studied. On the other hand, you may feel that these examples do not compare like with like and that other extracts might have suggested closer affinities between Enlightenment and Romanticism.

The texts which you have studied in this course are often complex composites of characteristics, sometimes blending Enlightenment with Romanticism, or sometimes reducible to neither. The Soane Museum functions most effectively perhaps as testimony to the richness of the cultural cross-currents in which these texts were formed. Just as there were signs of an emergent Romanticism prior to the Romantic era, so the values of the Enlightenment persisted into the nineteenth, twentieth and twenty-first centuries. Today we are probably all aware of a number of individuals or examples of cultural production and practice that continue to play out the competing values of both movements.

References

Anderson, M.S. (1985) *The Ascendancy of Europe 1815–1914*, 2nd edn, Harlow, Longman.

Blake, W. (1982) *The Complete Poetry and Prose of William Blake*, ed. D.V. Erdman, commentary H. Bloom, rev. edn, Berkeley, University of California Press.

Brookner, A. (2000) *Romanticism and its Discontents*, London, Viking.

Dolan, B. (2001) *Ladies of the Grand Tour*, London, Flamingo.

Eliot, S. and Stern, B. (eds) (1979) *The Age of Enlightenment*, vol.1, London, Ward Lock Educational.

Gardner, H. (ed.) (1991) *The New Oxford Book of English Verse*, rev. edn, Oxford, Oxford University Press.

Gibbon, E. (1998) *The Decline and Fall of the Roman Empire: 28 Selected Chapters*, ed. A. Lentin and B. Norman, Ware, Wordsworth Classics.

Halsted, J. (ed.) (1969) *Romanticism*, New York, HarperCollins.

Hampson, N. (1968) *The Enlightenment*, Harmondsworth, Penguin.

Hemmings, F. (1987) *Culture and Society in France 1789–1848*, Leicester, Leicester University Press.

Langenbucher, H. (ed.) (1937) *Deutsche Dichtung in Vergangenheit und Gegenwart*, Berlin, Bong & Co.

Mowat, R.B. (1937) *The Romantic Age: Europe in the Early Nineteenth Century*, London, Harrap.

Rousseau, J.-J. (1979) *Reveries of the Solitary Walker*, trans. P. France, Harmondsworth, Penguin (first published 1782).

Smollett, T. (1967) *The Expedition of Humphrey Clinker*, Harmondsworth, Penguin (first published 1771).

Soane, Sir J. (2000) *The Royal Academy Lectures*, ed. D. Watkin, Cambridge, Cambridge University Press.

Stendhal (1962) *Racine and Shakespeare*, trans. G. Daniels, New York, Crowell-Collier Press.

Sullivan, J.W.N. (1964) *Beethoven: His Spiritual Development*, London, George Allen & Unwin (first published 1927).

Thorlby, A.K. (1966) *The Romantic Movement*, Harlow, Longman.

Index

Page numbers in *italics* refer to illustrations.

148

148

148

148

Constable, John 20, 70
  and Delacroix's *Massacres of Chios* 77
  and Romantic art 80, 81, 121, 137
  The Sea near Brighton 121
Constantinople, Turkish victory at (1453) 94
Corregio, Antonio Allegri da 72
Courbet, Gustave 99
Cowper, William 111, 141
Coxe, Archdeacon William 129
Crace, Frederick & Sons
  and the Royal Pavilion 11, 24, 26, 27, 32
    Music Room 33, 40, 42
Cruikshank, George, *The Beauties of Brighton* 43–4

Dance, George 33
Danielli, William and Thomas, *Oriental Scenery* 33
Dante Alighieri, *Inferno* 74–5
David, Jacques-Louis 61, 74, 77, 127
  Andromache mourning Hector 62, 69
  The Death of Marat 128, 128
  Death of Socrates 63
  and Delacroix's *Massacres of Chios* 76
  The Lictors returning to Brutus the Bodies of his Sons 65, 91
  and neoclassical style 63, 65
Davy, Humphry 120, 122, 124
  and the Romantic artist 141, 143
  travel and the outdoors 131
De Quincey, Thomas, *The Confessions of an English Opium-Eater* 46–8, 87
deathbed scenes in paintings, and Delacroix's *Sardanapalus* 63, 65–6
Delacroix, Ferdinand-Victor-Eugène 5, 58–99
  Acrobats' Riding Class 90
  Alfred 86
  The Barque of Dante 73, 74–5, 85
  and Byron 82, 83, 88, 94, 95, 98
  and classicism 71–2, 74, 77–8, 77–9, 133
  colour in Delacroix's paintings
    The Death of Sardanapalus 69–70, 71
    Massacres of Chios 76–7, 96
    Mephistopheles appears before Faust 89
    and the Oriental 96
  The Combat of the Giaour and Hassan 95
  The Death of Sardanapalus 5, 7, 53, 60–79, 102–4
    and the 1827–8 Salon 60–1
    and David's *Andromache mourning Hector* 62, 69

deathbed in 65–6
Dionysiac and Apolline in 74
and distemper lay-in 70
female nudes in 66–7
and flossing 70
and the French government 61–2
and Gothic melodrama 86
horse in 97
and masculine fantasies 98
and modernity 89, 90–1
and neoclassical style 63–71
and the Oriental 92, 93–4, 96, 97–8
and Romanticism 77, 84–5, 99, 102–4, 130
and the Royal Pavilion at Brighton 86, 103–4
and Rubens 66–9
shadow in 70
education 71–2
and the exotic 97–8
family background 59
Faust lithographs 89
final years 99
and Géricault 72
Gothic novels and paintings of 86
Greece on the Ruins of Missolonghi 88, 96
and Gros 72–3, 75, 76, 77, 93
and individualism 126
and Ingres 70–1, 74
Liberty Leading the People 85, 88, 91, 111
Lion Hunt 97
Massacres of Chios 75–7, 89, 94–5, 96, 98
Mephistopheles appears before Faust 89
Michelangelo in his Studio 82
Moroccan journey 7, 59, 92, 93, 98, 99, 125
The Murder of the Bishop of Liège 71, 86
and the Oriental 6, 59–60, 96, 97–8
and politics 91
portrait of Paganini 82
and Romanticism 59, 77, 78–9, 79–92
  in the composition of paintings 134–6
  and the French monarchy 89–91
  and the Gothic 86, 87, 89
  and the grotesque 86–8, 89, 102
  and the 'impenetrable veil' 84, 136
  and modernity 88–91
  and the Oriental 98, 99
  and personal identity 125
  and the Romantic artist 81–4, 138–9
  and rough brushwork 80